New Life SERIES

Winning Friends for Christ

By Carolyn Sims

CONCORDIA PUBLISHING HOUSE • SAINT LOUIS

Edited by Thomas J. Doyle

This publication is also available in braille and in large print for the visually impaired. Write to Library for the Blind, 1333 S. Kirkwood Rd., St. Louis, MO 63122-7295; or call 1-800-433-3954.

Copyright © 1997 Concordia Publishing House
3558 South Jefferson Avenue, St. Louis, MO 63118-3968
Manufactured in the United States of America

3   4   5   6   7   8   9   10   06   05   04   03   02

Contents

Foreword

Always be ready to make your defense to anyone who
demands from you an accounting for the hope that is in you.
1 Peter 3:15 NRSV

"Always be ready." Those are important words. They provide at least three important learnings. First, it is possible to be
ready to share our faith. Second, you never know when the faith-
sharing opportunity will arise, so readiness is the order of the
day. Third, people need help and encouragement in that readiness.

This book is meant to be a tool for the Christian's readiness. It
gives wise and practical steps for the Christian to take. You will find
your time spent pondering and applying its points in your own witness to Jesus Christ. All of us are called upon to be witnesses for
Jesus Christ. 1 Peter 2:8–10 says all Christians by virtue of their Baptism are priests called to declare the mighty works of God. Acts
1:8 calls God's people witnesses. It is our duty and delight.

Congregations are finding that evangelism is not a program;
though programmatic emphases can assist evangelism. Evangelism
is not an event; though certain events can assist members in sharing their faith. Evangelism is a lifestyle. George Barna, head of
Barna Research Group and an astute watcher of the churched and
unchurched scene in America, writes that evangelistic congregations have this characteristic: "Their definition of success in evangelism is that people active in the church are intentionally and
obediently sharing their faith with nonbelievers" (*Evangelism That
Works,"* page 92). In other words, evangelism is sharing Christ in
the daily life of the believer. It is a lifestyle.

Yet, there is need for congregations to be more intentional
about the task of helping their members "always be prepared."
According to the Barna Research Group, only 12 percent of pastors could say their parishioners are effectively prepared to witness.
85 percent of the Christians who actively witness said they would

5

like to be better trained in evangelism. This book can be a valuable resource in that training.

A Partnership

This book represents a partnership between Concordia Publishing House and the Department of Evangelism Ministry of the Board for Congregational Services. Our goal is to work together to supply congregations and individuals with timely, effective, and faithful resources for training in evangelism. This book is one of a series in which the two entities are cooperating.

How to Use This Book

We hope that this book will be helpful in a variety of settings.

A weekly Bible class could take a number of weeks and work through this course. The text could be read ahead of time, reviewed in class, and the discussion questions could guide the class discussion.

A small group/home group could study this book over a period of meetings. This would be an excellent setting in which to take the time to encourage one another and support one another as participants take practical steps to be witnesses to Christ.

Two Christian friends could covenant to study this book together. They could help and encourage each other. Perhaps, most important, they could hold one another accountable to the learning and doing involved in this course.

Also, an individual could read, study, ponder, and apply the learnings of this book by herself or himself.

Congregations working hard at equipping their members for evangelism will find many more ways to use this book.

Words of Appreciation

What a joy it has been to work with CPH and Carolyn Sims on this project. We commend them for work well done. A special thanks to Carolyn for the fine work she did in writing these chapters. They reflect discussions from a daylong meeting and add creativity and personal touches to the notes of that day. Also, thanks to Rodney Rathmann at CPH for the work he has done and is doing in bringing this evangelism series into being.

It is our prayer that many will be blessed by their time in this book. Above all, we pray that all of us will grow in bold witness to our wonderful Savior, that many would come to trust His grace and that all glory will go to Him.

Rev. Jerry M. Kosberg, *Director*
Department of Evangelism Ministry
Board for Congregational Services
The Lutheran Church—Missouri Synod

Session 1
Plan Ahead

Who Me?

In the 1930s Dale Carnegie's *How to Win Friends and Influence People* became a best-seller. This book promised to make popularity possible for all—even for the social misfit. Carnegie introduced techniques and strategies that made people more likeable. The book and the philosophy it espouses are still popular today. The title conjures up in my mind, however, a rather bizarre scene.

Picture a carnival with the barker gathering a crowd like a fisherman trawling a stocked lake. "Step right up, ladies and gentlemen," he entices. "Everybody plays; everybody wins." The prizes to which he points, dangling on hooks in a colorful display, are not the usual stuffed pandas or Kewpie dolls; they are living human beings. "Pop the balloon, and win a friend," he intones. And one by one the flesh-and-blood trophies are taken down and added to the collection of whomever was skillful enough to "win" them.

The truth is, a life-and-death contest is being waged, and it is no game. The walls of Satan's den are lined with the souls of his apparent conquests. But Satan cheats! Those souls have been truly "purchased and won … not with gold or silver, but with His holy, precious blood and with His innocent suffering and death" (*Luther's Small Catechism* CPH 1986, p. 14).

They belong to Jesus. He paid the price for them, just as He did for you and me. But unless these people hear the Good News about their redemption from the power of sin and the devil, they cannot live as God intended them to—as a part of His family of faith.

Jesus wants your friends to be a part of the community of faith He has established. He has brought you into contact with other people so that all those He has already won can enjoy the blessings that are His to give. We, therefore, as Christians, view winning friends in a whole new light. We are in a position to *be* friends and to share the love of our best Friend, Jesus, with those who need to experience it.

The Bible calls this faith family by several different names. 1 Peter 2:9–12 describes it this way:

> But you are a chosen people, a royal priesthood, a holy nation, a people belonging to God, that you may declare the praises of Him who called you out of darkness into His wonderful light. Once you were not a people, but now you are the people of God; once you had not received mercy, but now you have received mercy. ... Live such good lives ... that [others] may see your good deeds and glorify God.

That's what this book is all about—letting your friends know that they have been won by the blood of Jesus Christ shed on the cross and that they, along with you, are a part of His family by God's grace through faith. That's the best news you could possible share.

Neighbors share all kinds of experiences. Often friendships blossom when children are small and parents gather in the front yard or street to keep an eye on them. Talk naturally centers around child-raising and common concerns. A new mother in the neighborhood asks who is the best pediatrician in town or where swimming lessons are given. People recommend schools and restaurants and pass on rumors about notorious teachers or crotchety homeowners. You share what you believe will be helpful to each other. If we are eager to point our friends to the nearest pizza parlor, couldn't we also point them to the love of our God?

We moved into a new neighborhood when our son was four years old. He immediately became well-liked among other neighborhood children. I was puzzled by his instant popularity until I watched him when he heard the ice cream truck one day. He ran to his piggy bank, which was much lighter than when we first moved in, and raided it for quarters to purchase treats for everyone. He was willing to pay the price in order to "win" friends. We, too, are called upon to make an investment in friendship so that we will be in a position to share something far more nourishing than ice cream—the Bread of life.

Many Christians consider Matthew 28:18–20 to be one of the most frightening passages in Scripture. It is called the "Great Commission," an awe-inspiring directive. "Go and make disciples of all nations, baptizing them in the name of the Father and of the Son and of the Holy Spirit, and teaching them to obey everything I have commanded you" (Matthew 28:18–20).

If Jesus truly expects us—*commands* us— to make disciples of all nations, then they—and we—are certainly in trouble. There is nothing in the world that would make me climb out of my comfortable home/family/church and risk the ridicule such a commitment might surely bring. Nothing on earth would move me to look like a religious fanatic to all my friends and preach "Jesus" to everyone. Besides, I'm terrible at that kind of thing. My faith is *personal,* after all. When I try to talk about God I get tongue-tied. The few times I've tried, I've blurted out some meaningless phrase that sounded stilted even to me. I'll do my part of winning the world by contributing to missions and praying for the *real* missionaries— you know, the ones Jesus called to that line of work. It makes good sense to leave such an important and complicated job to the professionals, doesn't it?

But wait, who was it that Jesus entrusted with the task of bringing the Good News of salvation to all the world? Matthew 28:16 introduces the cast—11 disciples. They were professionals, all right—professional fishermen, businessmen, and a government employee. And they were something else, besides. Matthew (who should know; he was one of them) tells us they were *doubtful.* They worshiped Jesus, yes, but even then, even after seeing Him dead and buried and alive again, some still had their doubts. Just like you—and me.

Jesus, of course, knew exactly what they were thinking. "Who, us? We know You better than anybody, and we're still not sure. To be honest, we're scared. Our lives are on the line because of You. We would much rather go quietly back to our boats and books. If You are the Messiah, You can commission rocks to spread the news. You don't need us. We really would rather not."

Jesus knew that nothing in the world could convince these frail followers of His to carry out the mission He had so boldly laid before them. So He empowered them with something *out* of this world. Acts 1:8 continues the story. "But," [Jesus promises,] "you will receive power when the Holy Spirit comes on you; and you *will* be my witnesses in Jerusalem, and in all Judea and Samaria, and to the ends of the earth" (emphasis added).

It was the Holy Spirit who changed these doubters into doers, these speechless gawkers into motormouths who *could not stop* the words from flowing from their lips. Listen to Peter and John in Acts 4:20, "We cannot help speaking about what we have seen and heard."

By the power of the Holy Spirit God took His followers off the mountain, lowered their upward-turned heads so they could see where they were going, and focused their attention on the "nations" He had in mind—their neighbors in Jerusalem, like the lame man at the temple gate; their countrymen in Judea, like Stephen and Paul; their irritating enemies like that demented Simon, the Samaritan sorcerer; and like the won't-take-no-for-an-answer Cornelius, who put Peter's new-found insight to the test by forcing him to act just when he was still in the middle of some radical divergent thinking about who was "clean" and "unclean."

If you have ever cringed at Jesus' commands, felt guilty because you just couldn't do what He expects, and yet wanted to express your love for your Savior and His people, take time now to hear what Jesus is telling you in His Word.

First, He says, as He proclaims so often in Scripture, "Don't be afraid. Lighten up! I will never ask more of you than I have already given you. I didn't send Paul to talk to the Ethiopian; he would have messed it all up. Philip was just right on that occasion. Can you imagine sensitive, reflective John mesmerizing the crowd on Pentecost? Motivational speaking was more along Peter's line. John wasn't ready to face that challenge yet. I had prepared him for other tasks. And you? You just might be surprised what I have in mind. Or, you might not be surprised at all. In fact, I think you will find that My plans for you make perfect sense. They should, after all, because 'you will receive power when the Holy Spirit comes upon you and you will speak of Me in …' "

Just as the disciples began in an area close to their hearts—Jerusalem, so we can focus attention on the place where our hearts live—among friends and acquaintances—among people we know and with whom we work—among those we care for and care about. Perhaps someday you will be called to faraway lands to tell the Good News about Jesus. But today, start here. It's where, by the direction of the almighty God, you are.

The devil loves to play I'm So Overwhelmed. There are billions of people on our planet who have never heard the name of Jesus and millions more who have heard His name but have not yet come to saving faith. *What good can I do? I am only one, and there are so many to tell!*

You may have heard the story about the boy and the starfish. His father observed the child picking up these sea creatures, which had beached themselves upon the sand and were left stranded until the next high tide. They would surely perish on the hot, dry beach. The boy resolutely picked them up one at a time and tossed each one back into the water. Each new wave, however, dropped more and more onto the land. "Can't you see it's futile?" admonished his father. "Even though you toss some back, more continue to come. Your efforts make no difference."

"It makes a difference to that one," replied the boy, as he tossed one more starfish back into the sea.

We may not be able to tell *every*one about God's love in Christ, but we are in positions to tell *some*one.

The purpose of this study is to identify who that someone is, to learn techniques for effectively communicating God's love to that person, to pray for that person, and to bring that person into fellowship with other Christians as the Holy Spirit works saving faith through the power of God's Word.

Do you have some doubts? You are in good company. You stand on the top of the hill with the original Eleven. Thank God! First, enjoy the view. You have an excellent vantage point.

Look back. Think about the week that has just past. Where were you seven days ago? Who was with you? What were you doing? What about the next day? And the next? Did you spend most of your time with fellow Christians or with unchurched neighbors and colleagues? It will be helpful to take a few moments if you are studying this book in a class setting to gather with one or two other members of the class and share with each other experiences you had during the week that caused you to interact with a person who is apparently unchurched.

The Unchurched

What does "unchurched" mean? We know that statistics tell us 12 million people in the United States describe themselves as "Lutheran." Yet Lutheran churches record a membership total of 8 million. According to a Gallup Poll, about 12 percent of the population are actively involved in established congregations. They attend church faithfully, give sacrificially, and serve willingly. Another 28 percent are members, but infrequently attend and minimally support the church. Forty-four percent fall into a category often called the "de-churched." They remember what church they went to as children. Often they consider themselves Christian but are disconnected from any organized church. This group is particularly open to the nurturing of a Christian friend. They are looking for a faith that works, and the place they look is at the lives of people who profess to be Christians. The last 16 percent are firmly unchurched. They have little or no interest or background in Christianity and may, in fact, be antagonistic to Christians and the Christian faith.

For the purpose of this study "unchurched" is defined as a person who has no apparent connection with a Christian church—a church which proclaims Jesus as true God, our Savior, and the only way to heaven. The "de-churched" group mentioned above would fall into this category. We need to be careful not to judge what is in another person's heart. Only God looks there. We see only what happens on the outside of a person's life. Based on what we observe and hear, we can form an opinion as to whether or not that person attends church regularly and professes a Christian faith. What does that person do on Sunday morning? What kind of language is typically used? How are problems and conflicts dealt with? Has this person reached out to you with questions and concerns that indicate a need for the forgiving love and security that Christ offers? Rather than look for broken commandments, look for signs of broken relationships between that person and others and between that person and God—perhaps even a broken heart within that person which only God can heal. You will be able to recognize that person easily; that person will look a lot like you. That's why God has brought you into the same neighborhood, family, or workplace. Can you picture that person now? Are there more than one? Do you need to look more carefully? Do you see someone you would rather overlook?

Where to Find the Unchurched

Where should you look? There are basically four basic places. First, look at the people you already spend time with—your family and close friends. These are the people with whom you share confidences. You see them weekly, if not daily. You like each other. You discuss movies and books and fears and dreams.

Next, watch for acquaintances whose paths cross yours regularly, but not closely. These are people you know at work or the neighbors down the street to whom you wave as they pick up the newspaper and you drive by on your way to church. You may have a standing appointment just after theirs at the hair salon or cheer with them at your child's soccer game. Sometimes they will make themselves known to you with a question or a particular concern. Sometimes you will notice or hear secondhand that they have specific needs or interests. Usually you consider them part of the scenery. You aren't sure what kind of car they drive, and you don't really care.

A third place to look is under the figurative rug. You are forced to deal with these people regularly, but you find them irritating. You have little in common. You speak only when necessary. Their children are a bad influence on yours. They are the neighbors who don't cut their grass. They are the business associates who make shady deals. They live blatantly hedonistic lifestyles. You don't want their car parked in front of your house.

One further place that needs to be scanned is within your own heart. To be honest, you know that there are people with whom it is extremely difficult for you to talk about your faith in Jesus. Often family members and close friends are the hardest to be open with. You have so much invested in these relationships you are reluctant to put them at risk by bringing up a potentially controversial subject. You don't want to be thought odd by the people whose opinions mean the most to you.

Marginal acquaintances present another problem. How do you get around to the subject of salvation when you are talking about who won last night's ball game? And why should you even want to encourage further contact with people you've spent years learning how to avoid?

Nevertheless, just for now, list these people individually and picture them in your mind. What specific needs do you know about? What are their strengths?

What gifts has God given them that He could use in His kingdom? What do you admire about them? What do you wish was different? Remember, it is not your intent to "fix" anyone. Even Christians have bad habits and irritating traits. You are identifying people with whom you can develop a relationship of camaraderie and trust so that, as a friend, you can share the Good News of Jesus, your Savior. Look, especially, for people who are going through transitions in their lives. During times of transition people typically look for something or someone stable.

Arrange the names you have thought of in a "web." Draw lines designating the ways in which you are connected. Are there other connections between any of the people you have identified? See the sample below.

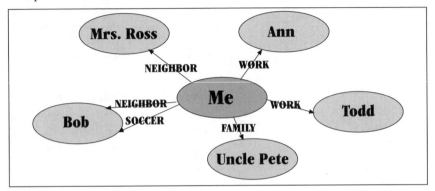

Pray for the people you have identified and pray for God's guidance so that you will be able to be a friend to a person who needs to hear about Jesus. Pray that you may overcome personal obstacles that would keep you from developing relationships. Ask for God's forgiveness for times you have focused on fears instead of faith. Pray for discernment and for power to know and do God's will.

Then choose one person on whom you are willing to focus. It may be that someone has already chosen you. Sometimes God works through ordinary circumstances to place His people (you) in the right place at the right time.

Tina and Walt welcomed newcomers Dee and Steve into the neighborhood. Steve's mother had worked with Tina years before, and Tina recognized Steve from a picture his mother had kept on her desk at work. Steve knew Tina had no interest in the church and, in fact, was antagonistic toward it. When Leanna invited Tina's daughter to a youth activity at the church, Tina allowed her to attend, and she had a great time. She began attending the youth activities regularly. The pastor sent a routine follow-up letter to the family, inviting them to attend church services, but Tina's response was "No way!" A month later Tina asked Dee (a congregational youth director), "Tell me about your job." Dee described her experiences and emphasized the importance of spiritual development. One Sunday Tina and Walt showed up at church. Then their daughter enrolled in Sunday school and the family began attending church more regularly. When Tina heard about the annual Women's Retreat, she wanted to go. On the list of things to bring was a Bible. Tina told Dee she did not own a Bible and asked what to do with it if she should purchase one. So Dee bought a Bible for her and showed her the basics of what it contained and how it was arranged. Dee was unable to attend the retreat, but Tina went on her own. She met more warm and welcoming friends, and grew to feel accepted and valued. Since then her children have been baptized and she has become a member of the congregation. All this began with a mom's picture of her son on her desk at work.

Tom and Anna were burned out on the church. They left a Roman Catholic congregation to experience the more lively contemporary worship practices of a nondenominational megachurch. Soon, however, they began to feel oppressed by all that was being required of them. They were expected to attend services several times a week and be involved in a small group which met midweek. They were intimidated into tithing and not allowed to participate in activities they had previously enjoyed, such as playing cards and attending dances as a couple. The demands drove them away from that church and from all churches. When they moved next door to Dee and Steve, they could tell immediately that Dee and Steve were Christians. Symbols on the door, active involvement in their congregation, and mutual acquaintances left no doubt. Tom and Anna enjoyed the company of Dee and Steve, but they made it clear that they wanted no part of religion. They did not want to talk about it; they did not want to be invited to attend any church functions. They said, "Please, don't try to evangelize us!" Dee and Steve continued to be neighborly, and the children continued to play together. Then 9-year old Leanna invited Tom and Anna's daughter to vacation Bible school for one week during the summer and to a monthly youth group which met at the church. Dee and Steve invited Tom and Anna for dinner shortly after vacation Bible school was over. In the middle of the conversation around the table Anna asked, "So, tell us about your church. What are the requirements? Do our children have to be baptized again? How much money will it cost us to join?" Dee and Steve gladly answered all the questions their neighbors raised. The family has joined them in church several times. They are not ready to make a commitment yet, but the care and concern of a friend has brought them into contact with the Gospel message of freedom from sin's control. They are on their way.

By now you may be asking yourself three basic questions:

1. What am I doing here?
2. Why am I doing this?
3. Who am I to be telling others about their relationship with God?

You are here because God has chosen you to be a friend. He has placed you in relationships with other people. He has made you His own through faith in the crucified and risen Jesus and empowered you to share the message of salvation with others for whom you care.

You are doing this because you really can't help it. Just as a plant grows toward the sun or water flows downhill, God has empowered and motivated you through faith to serve Him. Like Peter and John, once you start you will find that you cannot help speaking about what you have seen and heard. You are doing this because God has placed loving concern in your heart for your friends. Proverbs 17:17 reminds us, "A friend loves at all times." What better way to demonstrate that love than by introducing your friends to your best Friend, Jesus?

You are a redeemed child of God—no better than others, but equally holy in God's eyes, who has declared you perfect by Christ's blood shed on the cross. In fact, the reason your conversation about your Savior is effective is because you have so much in common with those with whom you interact. You can share your own moments of doubt and the assurance you were given, your own pain and the healing God brought, your guilt and the forgiveness in which you now live.

James Kennedy, in his book, *The Evangelism Explosion*, illustrates the importance of having the "right to ask." If you meet a person walking down the street and call out to him, "How's your kidney?" you would probably be met with shock and puzzlement. You may even be accused of rudeness and insensitivity. If, however, you are a doctor, and the man you meet is a patient you have been treating for a kidney infection, the question "How is your kidney?" does not seem so strange at all. You have earned the right to ask by virtue of your relationship with the other person. So it is in sharing the message of Jesus' forgiveness with others. Throughout my life I have been involved in numerous "evangelism programs." Some of these approaches involved knocking on doors and presenting a Gospel message to whomever answered. I participated in these programs because I felt I should. But I never felt comfortable carrying them out. Like the leader who shared his concerns, I prayed before I approached the first door and God answered my prayer—no one was home! I never saw many positive results from these calls, although the Holy Spirit could certainly use those methods, too, to accomplish His goals. I mostly felt embarrassed, inept, and frustrated. On one occasion we visited a secluded farm house in the middle of the Kansas countryside. It was sleeting, the ground was muddy, and we were miserable. We doggedly made our way to the door and were invited into a dark living room. A wet, smelly cat with matted hair came in with us and promptly jumped up into my lap, where it remained. The cat swished its soggy tail back and forth in front of my nose the entire time we were talking. I stoically put up with the discomfort so as not to offend the people who, obviously, thought highly of their pet. Finally, when it was time to leave, I stood up and the animal jumped to the floor. As we were saying good-bye the woman watched us go and remarked, "I wonder who that cat belongs to!" I had endured all that discomfort for no good reason. Often our efforts at sharing God's Word seem just as futile. *But,* when you have the right to ask, when you are a trusted friend and a familiar guest, your words are accepted and your interaction is welcome.

Getting Started

Resolve now to earn the right to ask at least one of the people you identified as needing to know about Jesus among your family or acquaintances. How do you decide which one? If you are still not certain, start with somebody obvious. Ask the Lord to direct you. Ask Him to send someone so open to His Spirit that you have only to fall into the relationship with ease. Once you have experienced the thrill of leading a friend to the Savior, you will be eager for your next "assignment."

Read the following examples from Scripture and identify who told whom about Jesus. What was the relationship that existed? Was it natural or intentionally cultivated? How did the person know whom to bring?

"Andrew, Simon Peter's brother, was one of the two who heard what John had said and who had followed Jesus. The first thing Andrew did was to find his brother Simon and tell him, 'We have found the Messiah' " (John 1:40–41).

"Philip, like Andrew and Peter, was from the town of Bethsaida. Philip found Nathanael and told him, 'We have found the one Moses wrote about in the Law, and about whom the prophets also wrote—Jesus of Nazareth' " (John 1:44–45).

"Then, leaving her water jar, the woman went back to town and said to the people, 'Come, see a man who told me everything I ever did. Could this be the Christ?' " (John 4:28–29).

"Then the father realized that this was the exact time at which Jesus had said to him, 'Your son will live.' So he and all his household believed" (John 4:53).

"But Peter kept on knocking, and when they opened the door and saw him, they were astonished. Peter motioned with his hand for them to be quiet and described how the Lord had brought him out of prison. 'Tell James and the brothers about this,' he said" (Acts 12:16–17).

"About midnight Paul and Silas were praying and singing hymns to God, and the other prisoners were listening to them. Suddenly there was such a violent earthquake that the foundations of the prison were shaken. At once all the prison doors flew open, and everybody's chains came loose. The jailer woke up, and when he saw the prison doors open, he drew his sword and was about to kill himself. … But Paul shouted, 'Don't harm yourself! We are all here!'… He brought them out and asked, 'Sirs, what must I do to be saved?' They replied, 'Believe in the Lord Jesus, and you will be saved—you and your household.' Then they spoke the word of the Lord to him and to all the others in his house. At that hour of the night the jailer took them and washed their wounds; then immediately he and all his family were baptized … he was filled with joy because he had come to believe in God—he and his whole family" (Acts 16:25–34).

Think about the following settings. With whom might you cultivate friendships in these areas?

Barber shop	Grocery store	Hardware store
Carpool	Service people	Fellow joggers/
Play group co-op	who come to	walkers/health
Bridge club	your home	club members
Gas station	E-mail	Doctor's office
Restaurant where	Travel agent	Church patio
you are a	Insurance	
"regular"	company	

To Consider and Discuss

1. Who did you identify as a friend with whom to share the Gospel?

2. Why did you choose this person?

3. What obstacles do you foresee that would hinder your relationship?

4. Whom can you enlist to help you develop this friendship?

5. When will you make an initial contact with this person?

6. What makes sharing the Gospel difficult for you?

7. How might you overcome these fears?

8. How did you become a member of the "priesthood of all believers"? As a "priest," what rights and responsibilities are yours?

Session 2
Prayer Power

Buyer's Remorse —

Are you acquainted with "Buyer's Remorse"? Buyer's Remorse is the feeling that sets in right after you have signed the contract for a new house or car, right after you have made a major commitment and you stop to think about the long-term ramifications. You panic. Your brain won't stop screaming, "What have I done?"

If you were serious about your commitment to develop a friendship with the goal of leading that person to Christ, if you have bought into the idea that God has called you to tell others about Him, by now you might be experiencing a form of spiritual "buyer's remorse." What have you done? How can you possibly carry it out? Is there any way to back out gracefully? The devil loves to play with your mind and soul.

Are you thinking,
- I'm too busy?
- I don't know enough about religion?
- No one would listen to me?
- I'll think about it for now and do it later?
- I don't know who to choose?
- I hate to get involved?
- Someone else could do it better?
- I must have been out of my mind?

Good! You have taken session 1 seriously and are confronting the first step of any successful venture: counting the costs. Remember, the disciples had their doubts, too.

This chapter will focus on dealing with those concerns. Buyer's Remorse sets in because you suddenly worry about the availability of resources or the value of your purchase. What if you lose your job? How will you make the payments? What if you find something you like better? Is the item you bought really the best?

God's Word speaks to both these concerns in the realm of your spiritual commitment to the task you have begun. First, He makes

21

available to you His unlimited resources of time, opportunity, motivation, and power through the study of His Word and the lifeline of prayer.

In this chapter we will identify specific things you can pray for and about. We will give examples of ways in which God has answered prayer in the past. And we will challenge you to put God to the test as He has invited you to do. Then we will celebrate His power at work in the lives of His people.

Perhaps you have already prayed for the strength and faith of St. Paul. There was a man committed to his Lord and to the task of telling the world about the Savior. How boldly he spoke! How fearlessly he encountered resistance! It was easy for him. He had the personality for it.

Read Ephesians 6:19–20: "Pray also for me, that whenever I open my mouth, words may be given me so that I will fearlessly make known the mystery of the gospel, for which I am an ambassador in chains. Pray that I may declare it fearlessly, as I should."

Could it be that even St. Paul grasped for the right words when he needed to speak? That he, too, was plagued by fear when faced with declaring God's Word in threatening circumstances?

In these short verses we get a glimpse of the human side of Paul. He worried about what he would say, totally dependent on God for whatever turned out successfully. And he knew it. He regularly tapped the same source of power which is available to you and me. He drew his strength and abilities from God as he studied God's Word and made us the resource of fervent and focused prayer.

First, St. Paul identified when he needed help—*whenever I open my mouth*.

Resolve, like Paul, to pray for opportunities to open your mouth and speak about Jesus. As you cultivate friendships, pray that every word you speak reflects the love God has for people. Whether you are speaking of spiritual or secular subjects, make the psalmist's prayer your own: "Lord, open my lips, and my mouth will declare Your praise" (Psalm 51:15). You do not know what statement or comment will make an impression on the person with whom you are talking.

Lisa became acquainted with Mrs. Long when her parents began giving the elderly lady a ride to church on Sundays. Mrs. Long was 83-years-old and nearly blind. It was Lisa's job to walk Mrs. Long back to her room in the nursing home after church each week. They chatted a little, but, frankly, Lisa could think of few things to say. When the time came for Lisa to go away to college, she walked Mrs. Long to her room for the last time that summer. "Good-bye," she said. "I'm leaving this week for school so I won't be here next Sunday, but I'll see you at Christmas!" Mrs. Long broke out in a huge smile. "You'll see me at Christmas," she repeated, and laughed out loud. Mrs. Long was no longer accustomed to such long-range plans. Her mind had been set on what she could no longer do. She had been living in depression and was waiting to die. Now she was waiting for Christmas and living with Christmas joy. Lisa had no idea that her simple comment could make such a difference in a person's life. God used the friendship between the two to bring peace to the heart of someone who desperately needed it. By the way, Lisa did see Mrs. Long again at Christmas, and for several more Christmases to come. They enriched each other's lives in ways only God could have directed.

Next, Paul prayed for words *to be given him*. Pray here for two things:

What to say and what *not* to say.

If life happened only according to a script, if only you could sit down, think it through, look it up, and determine just the right words in every situation, but life does not happen page by page. Life happens all at once. You are sitting at your desk and your secretary breaks into tears just as the phone rings. A police car brings your neighbor's son home in the middle of the night. Your mother-in-law's tests come back from the doctor showing a suspicious shadow on her lung. Your barber asks, "Just what goes on at that church of yours, anyway?" After stammering and blurting out whatever comes to mind, we usually think later about what we *should* have said. We play the tape over and over in our mind, but it always comes out the same. We feel guilty and inept. With Paul, pray for the right words at the right time. Receive God's forgiveness for verbal gaffes, but remember that God is a master at turning blunders into blessings. Keep talking; watch for new opportunities; bring up the subject at a later time to clarify or elaborate. And watch God at work through your words.

Mark made a thoughtless comment when he read an article about AIDS to his colleague, Fred, in the lunchroom. "Those people get what they deserve," he pontificated. Later he found out that

reader

Fred's brother had died of an AIDS-related illness. Mark was tempted to let the matter rest and chalk it up to experience, but later he saw Fred sitting alone and joined him. "I'm sorry for the remark I made the other day," he began. "I never meant to hurt you; it was really insensitive of me. I guess I have a lot to learn. I'm sorry about your brother. You must miss him a lot." Fred began to talk about his brother and the pain his illness and death had caused his family. God used Mark's initial blunder to open the door to further intimacy. Mark's acknowledgment of his own fault allowed Fred to speak of his own mixed feelings and fears. Mark became a trusted confidante who later had earned the right to speak about God's unconditional love for Fred and his family.

Often prayers for the power to remain silent shoot up like a barrage of arrows in the middle of a medieval battle. More than once I have bitten my lip as a reminder to keep my mouth shut. Clues that this approach is in order abound. I try to hold my tongue if the words about to come out of my mouth sound like,

- I told you so.
- If I were you,
- Don't you know …
- What in the world were you thinking?
- What's wrong with you?
- What you ought to do is …
- I would never …
- You always …
- You never …
- Why would you ever …

You get the picture.

Those phrases and others like them put the listener on the defensive and set you up as judge and jury. They close the door to any effective communication and revoke your right to ask. They hurt. They hurl obstacles in the path that will have to be dealt with later before you can focus on God's unconditional love and power.

Jesus' followers must have often wished they could call back the words they had uttered without thinking—words such as,

- "Hey ladies, *don't you know* Jesus is too busy to be bothered by those children. Get them out of here!" (Mark 10:13)
- "Don't worry, Jesus; the others may run away, but *I would never* forsake you." (John 13:3)
- "*If I were you, I'd* rain down fire and brimstone on these

ingrates." (Luke 9:54)

- "*You really ought to* set us up as your righthand men." (Mark 9:37)
- "*You should have* been here sooner; then my brother would not have died." (John 11:21)
- "*What in the world are You thinking?* Don't you know that if you go to Jerusalem your enemies will capture and kill you?" (John 11:8)

Despite their misspoken words, Jesus managed to accomplish His will. Pray that your words do not become an obstacle, but remember that God's will will be done. Hymn 371 *(LW)* "O God, My Faithful God" is a helpful prayer, which I encourage you to memorize and use in situations dealing with words.

> Keep me from saying words
> That later need recalling;
> Guard me lest idle speech
> May from my lips be falling;
> But when within my place
> I must and ought to speak,
> Then to my words give grace
> Lest I offend the weak.

Next Paul prays for courage so that he may speak *fearlessly.* Have you ever tried to talk yourself or somebody else into doing something by using the reasoning, "Come on—what's the worst thing that could happen?" That line of thought works for convincing yourself to ride a roller coaster, but when you apply it to Paul's life it isn't very encouraging. Listen to his accounting of "worst case scenarios":

> I have ... been in prison ... been flogged ... and been exposed to death again and again. Five times I received from the Jews the forty lashes minus one. Three times I was beaten with rods, once I was stoned, three times I was shipwrecked, I spent a night and a day in the open sea, I have been constantly on the move. I have been in danger from rivers, in danger from bandits, in danger from my own countrymen, in danger from Gentiles; in danger in the city, in danger in the country, in danger at sea; and in danger from false brothers. I have labored and toiled and have often gone without sleep; I have known hunger and thirst and have often gone without food; I have been cold and naked.

Besides everything else, I face daily the pressure of my concern for all the churches. (2 Corinthians 11:23–28)

No wonder Paul prayed so intently. He had, indeed, been there; done that. He had no illusions left that the task would be easy. He knew different. He was frightened and had a reason to be.

Have you had bad experiences in the past as you have attempted to share the news about Jesus with others? Have you been afraid to even try? Do you have a lot at risk—a marriage, a friendship, a promotion? Pray now for courage to speak fearlessly. 1 John 4:18 observes that "perfect love drives out fear." Be assured that God, who *is* Love, answers prayer. Pray for peace and confidence to act on God's promises and face the challenge He puts before you.

St. Paul mentions the *mystery of the Gospel*—the Good News of Jesus Christ. He is referring to the fact that the application of the Gospel message was "hidden" for many years and kept from the Gentiles. Now, however, it was revealed by God for all to know and understand.

Offer a prayer of thanksgiving that God has revealed His Word of forgiveness and grace to you. Thank Him for the people who have taught you about Him—parents, teachers, pastors, friends. And pray for those whom you tell. Pray that the Holy Spirit will open their hearts and minds to accept His Word and understand its power in their lives. The message of the Gospel—God's unconditional love and forgiveness for sinners—is foolishness to those who try to understand it rationally. Pray that the Spirit will work in the hearts of those people with whom you share God's Word so that they perceive it through the eyes of faith and so that they come to believe and accept it. Much of the language of Christianity is meaningless to those who have not been in contact with the church. Words such as *redemption* and *sanctification,* even *sin* and *grace* sound like a secret code for the in-crowd. Pray that God would enable you to share His love in Jesus by using words that make sense to the listener. Jesus did that when He spoke in parables, using everyday images and examples. When He said that He is the Bread of life, people thought about what was necessary to sustain life. When He spoke about a shepherd's concern for his flock, people understood more clearly God's love for His people and their dependence on Him. Pray for insight into ways of "translating" God's Word into the language of your listener.

Finally, Paul identifies himself as God's *ambassador*. An ambassador does not speak his own words. He speaks only the words of the one who has sent him as his representative. Pray that God will keep your message focused on the words He has given you to say. Ask for strength to avoid side issues that are of no real importance. Political issues, social issues, even denominational issues can get in the way of your real message—Christ crucified. Can a person be a Christian and support the Republican party? Can a person be a Christian and support the Democratic party? Can a person be a Christian and believe in evolution? Can a person be a Christian and drink beer? While Scripture contains many precepts which are relevant to our daily lives, remember to focus on that which is of eternal consequence. There will be time later to grow in commitment and understanding. Begin with the clear and simple truth of the Gospel.

When I was in college I attempted to share God's Word with an unchurched friend who was an engineer. "Okay," he challenged. "Let's start at the basics—I believe in science; I could never accept the Bible's story about creation." Creation is *not* the basics. Once a person believes in Jesus as the Savior from sin and His resurrection from the dead, matters of creation, miracles, and interpretations about women's place in the church begin to make sense. Pray that God will keep you focused on what is necessary for salvation.

The Needs and Concerns of Others

So far we have prayed for opportunities, for words, for courage, for discernment, and for focus. All of these factors relate to our own readiness and ability to communicate. Now it is time to focus on the needs and concerns of those with whom we seek to foster relationships.

What Paul desired for himself, he also desired for others. In 1 Timothy 2 he directs, "I urge, then, first of all, that requests, prayers, intercession, and thanksgiving be made for everyone … This is good, and pleases God our Savior, who wants all men to be saved and to come to a knowledge of the truth" (vv. 1–3). We also have God's promise in James 5:16: "The prayer of a righteous man is powerful and effective."

Who is a "righteous man"? Anyone whom God declares righteous by grace through faith. That means you and me, although our assessment of ourselves would be more critical. Through His perfect life and death on the cross, Christ has made us perfect in God's sight. That is what it means to pray "in Jesus' name." We are able to approach God with total confidence, knowing that He will hear and answer us as He has promised, according to His will. And what is His will? He wants to save all people so that they may come to a knowledge of the truth.

Coming to a knowledge of the truth is exactly what we have in mind for the friends for whom we pray. So pray boldly. Our Lord invites requests. Request opportunities to exhibit friendship. Request time to spend with others. Request creative ideas for making connections. What is your heart's desire? Lay it before your heavenly Father, who knows your heart, and leave your request in His capable hands.

Intercessions are prayers offered on behalf of somebody else. They are the prayers you pray for others. Focus, now, on the person you seek to befriend. Think about that individual's personality and needs. If you know that person well, this step will be easy. If you have chosen a more marginal acquaintance, you may have to do some research. Observe and listen. If that person has talked with you about a particular concern, say that you will pray about it.

Margaret was worried about a job interview scheduled for 2 P.M. on Wednesday. She told her friend Joyce about her concerns. "I'll pray for you at two on Wednesday," promised Joyce, and she did. Margaret was touched. No one had ever, to her knowledge, prayed specifically for her before. The interview went well, and from then on Margaret could not think about her new job without connecting it in her mind with the prayer of her friend. As other needs arose, she found herself asking Joyce to "do that prayer thing" again. Joyce was able to talk with Margaret about her relationship with God, who is able and willing to answer the prayers of His children.

It is also possible to pray for others without them ever knowing. Pray that God will make them receptive to the Holy Spirit. Pray for others who you know share the Gospel with friends or family, too.

Which is better, letting others know you are praying for them or keeping it to yourself so as not to make them feel uncomfortable? It depends on the person and the situation, of course. Often people are reticent to share their prayer experiences. One elderly woman who had been in the same Bible class for years suddenly pointed to her friend across the room and spoke up, "I prayed for you every day you were in the hospital last week."

"Well, for goodness sake!" the friend responded. "Why didn't you tell me? It would have helped my morale if I had known."

A student from England received a telegram notifying her of her father's death. It was Christmas vacation, and most of the students had gone home for the holidays. One classmate noticed the girl's distress. As she left the dining hall that night she stopped to tell her she would be praying for her. Later she learned that she was the only person who had acknowledged the classmate's loss. The two girls became close friends, based on this initial connection.

When my father died, I called my workplace to leave a message that I would not be able to keep an appointment for that afternoon, since I was at the hospital with him. Later I received a Scripture-based sympathy card from the woman whose appointment I had missed. That act of thoughtfulness touched me deeply. I know she was praying for me during that time of need.

When you tell others you are praying for them, be aware that God's plan may not coincide with your desires. If you pray for the healing of your friend's child and the child dies, be ready to discuss the feelings of anger and bitterness that may result. God can stand up to any test. Pray that He would use times of such intense pain to bring about faith and healing as you focus on His words of comfort and peace.

Keep on praying. Form a partnership with others in this class and pray for each other and each others' relationships. Pray for your pastor and the teachers in your church. Ask that God will bless their efforts to communicate His saving love. Ask your pastor what, specifically, he would like you to pray about on his behalf. Tell his wife you are praying for her.

Finally, as Paul concludes, give *thanks* for the answers to your prayers. When God's answer is yes, rejoice and share the news. When God's answer is no, thank God for being wiser than you are and ask for faith to trust Him. Share your prayer experiences with others and encourage each other in prayer. Invite others now to tell the best prayer stories they've got. You will be amazed at God's power and goodness.

The story is told of St. Augustine's early years. He rejected his Lord and the church and indulged in a life of sin and rebellion. His mother, Monica, however, never stopped praying for him, and in God's good time, her prayers were answered. Is there a prodigal in your life? In the life of your friend? Keep praying, knowing that the end of the story is in God's hands.

It is helpful to make a "prayer list." Keep a notebook or index card with you throughout the day and jot down prayer ideas. Record, also, answers to prayers as you observe them. Add them to your list of thanksgivings.

You will find that the more you pray, the more natural prayer will become. God uses His gift of prayer to energize you, the pray-er, as well as to direct His blessings on the one for whom you pray. In prayer, through the intercessions of the Holy Spirit, we call upon God to execute His mighty deeds. He acts in our hearts, strengthening us as we see Him at work in our life and in the lives of others.

In fact, when you have reached the end of your spiritual rope, when you can no longer find the words to pray for one more second, the Holy Spirit steps in and actually prays on your behalf. We read in Romans 8:36: "In the same way, the Spirit helps us in our weakness. We do not know what we ought to pray for, but the Spirit himself intercedes for us with groans that words cannot express. And he who searches our hearts knows the mind of the Spirit, because the Spirit intercedes for the saints in accordance with God's will."

Imagine it! The Holy Spirit, God Himself, makes our prayers "right" and answers them.

Four-year-old David's ears perked up in chapel when the pastor began to pray for his younger brother, Ricky. Ricky had been diagnosed with leukemia. David wasn't sure exactly what leukemia was, but he knew his brother was very sick and that he could die. As the pastor prayed, David clenched his folded hands together into a tight fist. He scrunched his eyes shut and tensed every muscle of his body, straining to pray as "hard as he could."

That's the way the Spirit prays for us and for those we pray about. He focuses that intensity on the needs and concerns which we bring before God's throne.

Jesus Himself taught us how to pray in the Lord's Prayer recorded in Matthew 6. Try praying for others specifically as you pray these familiar words. Include the name of the person for whom you are praying on the blank lines.

- Our Father *(Father of _____ and me)* who art in heaven.
- Hallowed be Thy name. *(Let _____ come to know Your name and honor it.)*
- Thy kingdom come. *(Let Your kingdom of grace come to the heart of _____. Live there as King.)*
- Thy will be done on earth as it is in heaven. *(It is Your will that _____ come to the knowledge of the truth. You died to make _____ Your own. Accomplish Your will now in _____'s life.)*
- Give us this day our daily bread. *(Provide according to Your will all that is necessary for _____'s life. Continue to supply all needs of body and soul.)*
- And forgive us our trespasses as we forgive those who trespass against us. *(Let _____ know that You are a God of forgiveness and mercy. Take away all guilt and let _____ live as Your ransomed child. Move _____ to also share Your grace with others.)*
- And lead us not into temptation. *(Protect _____ from Satan's influence and lies.)*
- But deliver us from evil. *(Cover _____ with the shadow of Your powerful wing.)*
- For thine is the kingdom *(_____ and I are a part of it)*
- And the power *(You can do it!)*
- And the glory *(thank You!)*
- Forever and ever *(together with You in heaven for all eternity).* Amen. *(You will do it. Amen!)*

Pray now, before you begin your ambitious task. Pray often, as your friendship unfolds. Pray later, when all has been said and done. Look forward to the time when you and your friend will pray together to the God who will accomplish His good work in you to the glory of His holy name.

We began this session by talking about "Buyer's Remorse." God assures us there is no need to be concerned about the resources available to us through prayer. And what about the value of the task to which we are committed? What is a human soul worth?

It was worth the life of God's own Son. Its value lasts throughout eternity. It has been entrusted into your care according to God's plan.

You have not been swindled into some slick deal by a fast-talk-

31

ing salesman. You have been called by the mighty God to give away what He has already given you in full measure.

Count the costs. Gather the resources. Proceed with caution, yet also with confidence. Replace "remorse" with "resolve." For God has promised that *your* prayer is powerful and effective.

Now pray for each other as you work toward your goal.

To Consider and Discuss

1. Tell about a time you prayed for someone secretly. Why did you choose to do so? What was the result?

2. Who prays regularly for you? How does it help?

3. Tell about a time God answered your prayer in a positive way.

4. Tell about a time God answered your prayer differently from what you had hoped. What was the result?

5. When did you first learn to pray? Who taught you? Thank God for that person.

6. Ask someone to be your prayer partner. Discuss specific needs and concerns and pray for each other regularly. If

possible, let the other person know precisely when you will be praying.

7. Thank God for three blessings which are of great value to you. Ask Him to use those blessings for the benefit of others in His kingdom.

8. Pray for someone you don't like very much. Keep praying for that person. Note whether or not your feelings and attitudes change. Why did they, or why didn't they?

Session **3** Person to Person

It has been said that people don't care what you believe if they don't believe that you care.

This session is about caring. It is about enhancing your relationship with another person so that person knows you care and so that you can, as a true friend, share the most important aspect of your life—your faith in Jesus, your Savior.

Be careful, here, to understand that you are not setting out to *act* like a friend. You are setting out to *be* a friend. You are intentionally cultivating a genuine relationship with another. In the process, both of you will be called upon to sacrifice, and both of you will benefit.

Consider these scenarios:

Scenario 1

A man was traveling from Jerusalem to Jericho and fell among thieves who robbed him of all that he had and left him lying by the side of the road. Before long a member of the church came by and saw the man lying there.

Chuck: Hello, there! I'm Charlie and I'm a member of First Lutheran Church.

Fred (Injured man): *(Groans)* Mmmm.

Chuck: Speak up, man, God helps those who help themselves, you know. You look very … dirty! If you'd clean up a bit you could come to my church. We have a parish-nurse program that could be of some real help. How does that sound?

Fred: Well, I could use some help all right, but I don't think I could …

Chuck: Of course you could. Just set your mind to it. That's what I do. Once I was injured worse than you, and I turned out okay.

Fred: Good for you. It's just that I can't seem to get my legs moving.

Chuck: What were you doing on this road, anyway? Everybody

34

knows you're a target for trouble along here. Did they get all your money? I only travel with the bare necessities, and I leave my credit cards at home. Next time you should, too.

Fred: Uh, yeah. *(He tries to move.)* Ow!

Chuck: When I'm having trouble, I pray about it. You do know how to pray, don't you? You know … confession, supplication, intercession, and all that? Didn't your mother ever teach you what's important? The Bible says, "Bring up a child in the way he should go and when he is old he will not depart from it." It's pretty obvious *some*body didn't get brought up in the way he should go. I guess you could just go to the Bible bookstore when you get to Jericho and look in the prayer section.

Fred: I don't *want* to go to the Bible bookstore. I don't *want* to read a prayer. And I don't *want* any part of your church or your God! I can take care of *myself!* (He limps away.)

Chuck *(Calls after him):* Hey, wait a minute. Here's a tract! Call the pastor if you need anything. *(To himself)* I guess you just can't help some people. That's the last time *I* try to share my faith!

Scenario 2

A man was traveling from Jerusalem to Jericho and fell among thieves who robbed him of all that he had and left him lying by the side of the road. Before long a member of the church came by and saw the man lying there.

Charlie *(rushes to his side):* Are you okay? Shall I call 9-1-1?

Fred: I'm not sure. Just give me a minute to get my bearings.

Charlie: What happened? *(He takes off his coat and puts pressure on a cut.)*

Fred: I guess I should have known better. I know this route is dangerous; it's just that I was in such a hurry to get home.

Charlie: It's important for you to get home right away?

Fred: Yes. My wife called from the hospital. Our little girl was running a high fever so she took her in. I wanted to be there.

Charlie: I'll help you get going as fast as you can. Let's see. It looks like the bleeding stopped. Did they get all your cash?

Fred: Every penny—and my credit cards.

Charlie: Where do you live?

Fred: Jericho—the Sycamore Creek section.

Charlie: I can go that way. Come on. Do you want to see a doctor first?

Fred: I just want to get home. Do you have any kids?

Charlie: Just one. In fact, I'm on my way to pick her up from a youth night at my church. I'll call from the hospital to tell her I'll be late. She'll be fine.

Fred: She'll probably worry.

Charlie: She knows she's in good hands until I get there. Say, I bet your daughter is pretty scared. Would it be all right if I prayed for her—and for you and your wife?

Fred: Pray? Sure. I guess it can't hurt. It's been a long time since I prayed about anything. Thanks. By the way, my name is Fred. I don't know what I would have done if you hadn't come along. Where in Jericho do you live? Maybe we could get together sometime.

Jesus' question, after telling a similar story, was, "Which of these was a neighbor to the man who fell into trouble? We would ask, "Which of these was a *friend?*"

What do you think happened next in Scenario 2? Charlie opened the door to building a relationship between himself and the man he helped. Let's take a look at how he went about it.

First, he took the initiative. He *saw a need* and went into action. Fred was obviously in trouble. Charlie didn't just talk in vague generalities or offer a generic "Let me know if there's anything I can do." He stopped, assessed the situation, and put pressure on the wound.

At the same time, he *listened* to what Fred was telling him. He listened with his heart and learned, first, that Fred did not need any further medical treatment. But even more important, he listened to the meaning behind Fred's words. He reflected to Fred the real message that was conveyed, "It's important for you to get home right away." That gave Fred a chance to say yes and an opportunity to say more about himself and his needs. Charlie didn't use "church" words and he didn't preach about what Fred *should* have done or not done. He merely shared the man's feelings of love for his daughter and provided practical help. Note how he was able to share the fact that he, too, had a daughter—and that he had a connection to a church. Father-to-father they spoke about their daughters' fears. Charlie felt comfortable, then, to offer to pray for Fred's daughter. Still, he did not push; he asked permission. This comment, too, evoked further conversation from Fred, and Charlie found out that Fred probably had some experience with the church in the past. ("It's been a *long time* since I prayed about anything.") The word *Thanks,* indicated he was not antagonistic. Charlie planted in Fred's mind the fact that church was a place where people were "in safe hands." Fred was feeling quite good about all this; in fact, it was he who took the initiative of seeking further contact with his new-found "friend."

This encounter was only step 1 in building a relationship which could lead to Fred's inclusion as an active member of God's family, but every relationship begins somewhere. Charlie and Fred were off to a good start.

As you cultivate a friendship with the person you have identified, think, first, about the status of your relationship right now. On a scale of 1 to 10, with 1 being a mere acquaintance and 10 being a close family member, where does your relationship fall?

If your relationship is 5 or lower, are you willing to find ways of becoming more involved on a day-to-day basis? If so, here are some suggestions:

1. Observe and listen to discover that person's special interests, hobbies, and activities. How and where does that person spend time?
2. Which of these interests and activities do you have in common?
3. Strike up a conversation about those interests.
4. Make plans to participate together in enjoying them at a particular date or time. Think about when you first noticed your future spouse. How did you go about getting better acquainted? Use the same techniques.
5. Pray for that person regularly. Ask that God would give you opportunities to develop a friendship and that He would provide ways in which you could share your faith.
6. Have fun together!

As you move into the 6–10 range of closeness, continue to pray for your friend and your friendship. You will find even more ways of nurturing the relationship that exists.

1. Send a card on special occasions or just a humorous card for no reason at all which speaks to a common interest.
2. Invite your friend to your own family events. Get to know each other's spouses, friends, and children.

3. Go to lunch together.
4. Help when needed with big and small needs.
5. Ask for help with your needs.
6. Talk about feelings and concerns.

Remember, you are not manipulating someone into a relationship for ulterior motives. You are building a relationship of genuine care and friendship. You are involving yourself in the church's "ministry." A "minister" in this sense, is a person who serves. Jesus observed that anyone who gives so much as a cup of cold water to a little child in His name is really serving God Himself. Caring about others in Jesus' name is what you are doing here. You are Jesus' arms and heart with which He shows His love to His people.

St. Paul had similar goals. He describes his actions in 1 Corinthians 10:31–11:1.

> So whether you eat or drink or whatever you do, do it all for the glory of God. Do not cause anyone to stumble, whether Jews, Greeks, or the church of God—even as I try to please everybody in every way. For I am not seeking my own good but the good of many, so that they may be saved. Follow my example, as I follow the example of Christ.

Making friends takes time, and it involves risks. Your friendship style may be different from that of others. Perhaps you enjoy attending concerts and plays. Don't expect to suddenly take up hang-gliding and bungee-jumping in order to cultivate a friendship. Even if you and your friend are quite different, seek out common ground, common interests and activities. God will show you the way. You must remain who you are. *You* are the one God has in mind.

If your attempts to be friendly are met with cool rebuffs, back off. Building trust takes awhile. Just keep caring and keep praying. The right moment will come. It may be God is leading you elsewhere. Be open to His direction; show His love and concern to *all* with whom you come into contact. But you will not have the time or energy to concentrate your efforts on *every*one. Remember, your goal for now is to choose one person to work with in a special way.

It is important to remember that friendship is a *process,* not a destination. As you continue to befriend and show loving care, you are successful—whether or not you ever hear that person confess faith in Jesus as Savior or see that person join a Christian church. The results are in God's hands. It is your commitment to be a friend.

Knowing that the results are in God's hands frees us to continue with confidence, following God's directive to love others as He loves us. We know that God will accomplish His will, in His own good time.

How long does it take? It depends on the people and on the circumstances. Dramatic events could forge a solid bond within hours or even minutes.

Flight 102 was approaching Detroit when the captain announced, "We are experiencing some difficulty with the landing gear." No one heard much more than that. A child started to wail. A passenger in the front of the cabin began screaming, and Nora, on her way to a church-related conference, glanced at the woman sitting next to her, who was sobbing hysterically. "Aren't you scared?" the weeping woman asked. "We're going to crash!" Nora's white knuckles clenched the armrest in a death grip. "Yes," she admitted. "This is one of my worst fears. But I do know that we are all in God's hands. I'm praying right now for His help and for courage to face whatever happens." In the next few minutes, with chaos breaking all about them, the two women spoke of family and friends, of joys and regrets. Nora prayed for them both and held her new friend's hand tightly within her own. She spoke of her certainty of heaven because of Jesus, her Savior, and together the two women closed their eyes and waited.

The pilot's voice broke the tension when he announced a few moments later that the landing gear was in place, and the crisis was over. Nora and her seat-mate smiled at each other and exchanged names and addresses. There was so much more that the woman wanted to ask, and so much more that Nora wanted to tell. They corresponded for months and continued to build on a friendship born in a split second of emotion.

Other relationships take months or even years to cultivate. No one knew "the dog lady," who lived at the end of the street very well. She waved as she passed the neighborhood children when she walked her two Scottish terriers every evening, but then she would retire to the recesses of her tiny house and not be seen again until the next evening. Marge always meant to take her a piece of pie left over from a family picnic or invite her to dinner some day. But she rarely saw her outside, and she didn't want to intrude. The woman probably napped most of the day anyway. Sometime soon she would definitely go over there and get acquainted. The ambulance pulled up to the curb about 10 o'clock in the evening. Marge wouldn't have seen it except she was just arriving home after a late meeting at church. She watched as the paramedics carried the frail woman out the door and prepared her for transport to the hospital. "My dogs," she cried. Who will take care of my babies if I am not here?"

"We'll send someone, Lady," soothed one of the medics. But the woman continued to fret.

Marge walked to the stretcher and took the woman's hand. "I'll watch after your dogs," she promised. What are their names?" She found out where the woman would be taken and called on her the next day. The woman, who was not accustomed to so much attention, could only smile gratefully. Over the next few months Marge visited Mrs. Mays regularly. She learned that the woman had been a schoolteacher for 30 years and had traveled all over the world. She had never married, but loved all the children she had known all those years. Marge introduced her to her own grandchildren, who loved to play with the dogs and investigate the many souvenirs Mrs. Mays had accumulated on her travels. "I thought I had no more to give," the woman explained. "The children seemed so frightened of me, I didn't want to push." She loved to hear Marge's grandchildren read to her, which they did quite frequently. Along with magazines and books, Marge sent along some devotional booklets, and she and Mrs. Mays began to discuss them together. When Mrs. Mays passed away the following year, Marge knew that her new old friend was in heaven with her Savior. What had taken her so long to take the first step?

Listening Skills

Probably the most important tool for developing a caring relationship is the ability to listen in open, nonjudgmental ways. Real listening involves an openness and concentration on the other person. Look the person in the eye, avoid distractions, and pay attention. Have you had the experience of speaking to someone, only to have them look past you, obviously watching for someone else? Three-year-old Theresa wanted to chat with her mother about her day at preschool. Mom, busy preparing dinner, continued setting the table while Theresa talked. "No, Mommy," protested the child. "Listen to me with your eyes!" She wanted and needed her mother's undivided attention. Like Theresa, all people need to feel they are important enough to be listened to directly.

Often people say much more than their mere words. Every husband knows that when he asks, "What's the matter?" and his wife sighs, averts her eyes, and answers, "Nothing," *nothing* means "something." He had better find out what is really going on in her mind. Pay attention to facial expressions and body language as you listen. With a little practice you will be able to discern hidden, yet significant, meanings behind the words.

One way to listen effectively is to reflect back to the speaker the feeling behind the words spoken or to ask questions which "scaffold" on the information first given.

The most revealing questions are open-ended rather than closed. For example, your friend enters the room in tears and shouts, "Mr. Reynolds just bawled me out for coming back late from lunch yesterday! I worked until six to finish the project, but he wouldn't even listen." If you ask, "Do you think he was being unfair?" the only alternatives are yes or no. If you say, "That must have been really frustrating," your friend can continue to vent her feelings.

"Did you read the book I gave you?" is not as helpful as, "What did you think about that book I gave you?"

It is also helpful to ask questions that clarify. "I feel wonderful!" can be expanded by the question, "What makes you feel so good today?" Avoid why questions because they generally imply judgment. "Why did you miss our luncheon date yesterday?" is accusatory. "I missed you yesterday at lunch," opens the door for an explanation as well as making the person feel cared about.

Sometimes it is necessary to stop and think about a person's words rather than reply immediately. "My life is in shambles and my wife just left me" does not require a quick "That's too bad; here's what you ought to do." Let the person know you, too, are overwhelmed by the implications of those words. You are realizing the impact and will respond when you have pulled your thoughts together. Allow time to share feelings for and with each other. Likewise, allow the other person time to be silent for a few moments when necessary. It is tempting to fill every conversational lull with "noise." Sometimes shared silence speaks volumes.

In order to clarify and validate the other person's feelings, reflective or "active" listening is beneficial. Although this technique may seem artificial at first, with a little practice it becomes a natural response. It diffuses highly volatile emotions and encourages the speaker to continue to talk. It also is a check to see if you are understanding the other person correctly. Reflect content, feelings, and concerns.

William J. McKay, in *Me? An Evangelist?* (St. Louis: Stephen Ministries, 1992), provides several examples of how reflective listening works in day-to-day life.

Possible reflective responses include the following:
- You're wondering if …
- It sounds like you're feeling …
- As I understand it, then, your plan is to …
- As you saw it, the situation was …
- So at that point you were feeling …
- From all you've said, you seem the most concerned about …
- You are really concerned about …

Remember, you are not just parroting words. You are interpreting the feeling behind the words; you are clarifying the main point of what the other person is saying. Often, just knowing that you understand is enough to calm a person and free that individual to begin solving the problem. This type of caring builds trust and gives you the right to share your faith and hope.

An elementary school principal confronted an angry parent in her office. The parent was explosively upset about a comment made by his daughter's classroom teacher. He was loud and aggressive in his speech, waving his arms wildly, and demanding to be taken to his child's classroom. "Mr. Evans," began the principal, looking him in the eye and speaking in a calm voice, "You feel very angry about what happened to your daughter."

"Yes, I'm angry," ranted the father. "I'm more than angry; I'm insulted that my child should be spoken to in that way. She has some pride, you know!"

"You would like to protect your child from being hurt like that."

"I want to protect her, but I can't always be there."

"You feel like you would like to be with her all the time."

"No, I know I can't be with her everywhere, but school should be a safe place."

"You would feel better if you could see that she is okay and that the teacher meant no harm by her remark."

"That's right."

"It sounds like you'd like me to talk to that teacher and straighten this out."

"Would you?"

"I'll do it now. Please wait here; I'll be right back."

The scenario continued, resulting in an apology by the teacher, who did not realize the effect her remark had on the little girl. The father later confided to the principal that he had come to school prepared to do bodily harm to the teacher. The principal's reflective and caring listening averted a possible act of aggression and began a positive relationship between parent and school.

William McKay records this conversation between two friends:

Annie: Well, it's finally happening. Sally's leaving for college tomorrow. I miss her already.

Susan: You're feeling lonely about Sally leaving.

Annie: Yes, I suppose I'm sad … but I don't think I should be. I remember my college days. They were a lot of fun. I'm sure she's going to have the time of her life.

Susan: So, you're feeling excited for her.

Annie: Yes, I'm happy for her, but sad for me. It makes me feel so selfish, but really I wish she wasn't going away.

Susan: This really hurts.

Annie: Yes, it does. It's hard to let go of your children.

By reflecting these feelings, Susan gave Annie permission to talk about unpleasant thoughts. Usually people are encouraged to cover up such negative feelings, but they can't be dealt with unless they are acknowledged. Susan showed great love and care for her friend.

Be careful to avoid these listening "traps."

1. Sending a quick-fix solution. It is usually enough to acknowledge the feeing expressed. Empathize. Your fast solution sends the message that this issue isn't complex or important after all. Besides, if your solution doesn't work, it will put a barrier between the two of you.

2. Evaluating and judging. Your friend doesn't need a scorecard. Don't set yourself up as a superior whose place it is to be critical. You are to model Jesus' *unconditional* love. Even the woman caught in the act of adultery was not criticized by the Savior. People will not share their feelings if they know they are being inspected. Even praise makes the person feel like someone in authority is handing out gold stars. Just listen.

3. Withdrawing. Once you commit to this relationship, you are love-bound to carry it through. You need to be dependable, not fickle. If there are issues you are not able to deal with (molestation, divorce, abuse), be honest with yourself and your friend. Do not resort to the "silent treatment" when your friend does not live up to your expectations. Great maturity is required on your part. Pray for this gift.

4. One-upping. Referring to a common experience communicates empathy, but don't go too far. It is extremely frustrating to tell someone your problem and then spend the next 15 minutes listening to that person relate similar experiences. Remember, your friend is the talker. You are the listener.

5. Diagnosing, analyzing, and labeling. Don't even think it. This is not the "frustrated man-hater." This is your friend who is hurting because of a distressing marital relationship. You are not a psychoanalyst. You are a friend.

A word of caution: Friendship implies *confidentiality*. It will be tempting to want to share with your spouse or classmates or other Christian friends the experiences you are enjoying as you engage in this process of building relationships. You are developing a friendship based on trust. Do not reveal anything that would be embarrassing or harmful to your friend. Safeguard your relationship by honoring its privacy and exclusivity.

Listening is one act of care through which Christian friends demonstrate God's unconditional love. There are many other ways to exhibit this concern. Concrete, caring deeds show that your words are not empty— that your love, and God's love which motivates it, is genuine. "Dear children," John implores, "let us not love with words or tongue but with actions and in truth" (1 John 3:18).

Betty was pregnant with her third child. She was experiencing severe morning sickness and started spotting in the third month. With two young boys to care for and a large house to keep up, she didn't know how she could follow the doctor's instructions to stay in bed for a couple weeks. Her husband had never had much to do with the church. He was a loving father, but his cooking skills were limited, and his business needed his full attention. Betty's co-workers at the church, where she worked part-time as a preschool teacher, went into action. They baby-sat for the boys, took over hot meals on a regular basis, and openly showed their care and concern. Each morning when husband Joe dropped off the boys he thanked the co-workers and gave an update on his wife's condition. The "couple weeks" turned into three, then four. The meals and care continued. Finally Betty was able to return to work, and the following July her baby girl was born healthy and fit. Betty had been praying for her husband for years. He had never been antagonistic to the church; he had just never seen the need to belong. He was a rational man, who needed to see things make sense. After his wife's pregnancy, however, Joe began attending church with his family. He came to the pastor's instruction class and expressed the desire to be a Christian, but his intellectual honesty still held him back. If, he said, the Holy Spirit works the miracle of faith through Word and Sacrament, he would listen to the Word and participate in the Sacrament of Baptism so that the miracle of faith could be generated in him. And that is exactly what happened. What had drawn him to the place where God made him His own? It was the care that was shown to his family during their hard times. Their family faced other difficulties in the months to come. When they were forced to move to a smaller house, friends from the church helped them clean, paint, and pack. Joe now passes that care and concern on to others. He has chosen to be involved in the church's Scouting program. In that capacity he meets many boys and their fathers, who feel what he felt. Through the relationships he is developing, others are coming into the caring environment of God's people.

According to a recent survey by the Barna Research Group, on why people have come to Christ and the church, the following was found to be true:

Church sermon	13%
Evangelistic crusade	5%
Invited by the pastor	5%
Youth camp/event	4%
Through the Sunday school	4%
Physical healing	5%
Death of a relative or friend	4%
Invited by a friend or relative	44%
Other	16%

(From *The Barna Report*, by George Barna. Jan/Feb 1996.)

Remember the statement made at the beginning of this chapter: *People don't care what you believe if they don't believe that you care.*

The corollary also seems to be true: *When people believe that you care, they care about what you believe!*

Friendships provide a natural network for sharing the Gospel.

New Christians who have discovered the joy of experiencing God's grace are eager to tell others. Their friends and relatives are the natural place to begin.

Friends and family are receptive to the words of people they trust.

Friendships allow for unhurried sharing of God's love in natural, everyday settings.

Friendships tend to involve whole families. When one member of a family comes to faith in Christ, it is often the beginning of a process that results in the entire family becoming involved.

It is amazing how rapidly a "web" of friend/family relationship can expand! Take a look at the following example of what happened in less than five years when one man, Ron Johnson, joined a Free Methodist church in Bellingham, Washington:

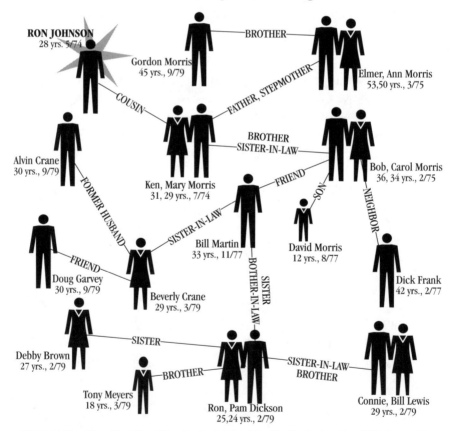

(Reprinted from *Growth: A New Vision for the Sunday School* by Charles Arn, Donald McGavran, Win Arn, Church Growth Press, © 1980. Used by permission.)

Times of Transition

There are times in a person's life when that person is especially open to the message of the Gospel. God's love and care are particularly appropriate during times of significant change (either positive or negative) and stress. Be sensitive to these times of transition in the life of the person you are befriending. These transitions include

- the death of a spouse;
- divorce;
- marital separation;
- jail term;
- the death of close family member;
- personal illness or injury;
- marriage;
- loss of employment;
- marital reconciliation;
- retirement;
- pregnancy;
- sexual difficulties;
- change in financial status;
- death of close friend;
- change in residence;
- son or daughter leaving home;
- holidays.

The most important factor to remember in establishing and living out your caring relationships is that you are modeling the *unconditional love* of Jesus.

Next-door neighbors Diane and Judy were talking over a cup of coffee after the children were off to school. "I don't know how I would have made it through these last few months without your friendship," began Diane.

"I know how devastating it was when Roy walked out on you," Judy said.

"Yes, but you were there to help with the kids and even lend me the money I needed to make the house payment that one month. I want you to know I really appreciate you."

"That's what friends are for."

"Judy, I know that you belong to a church and that you are a Christian. You never talk about it much, but I know it means a lot to you. I hope you don't mind that I'm just not into that kind of thing. I mean, it's okay for some people. It seems to be a big help to you. But everything has been happening so fast. I'm not ready to deal with religion right now. I just want to know. Have you been helping me because you want to convert me?"

Judy smiled. "Diane, I care about you because you are my friend. Yes, my relationship with God has a lot to do with who I am and why I do what I do. But you are my friend no matter what. My faith isn't in a religion; it's in a person—Jesus Christ. His love for me makes it possible for me to love you with no strings attached."

"Does that mean you'll still be my friend even if I don't want your religion?"

"You bet!"

Judy left the door open for further care. She modeled God's care for us who, "while we were still sinners, ... died for us" (Romans 5:8).

Several weeks later, Diane was at Judy's house again when the phone rang. It was bad news. Judy's mother had been killed in an automobile accident. Diane watched as Judy sat down and started to cry. After a moment she asked, "Doesn't it help? Your faith, I mean."

"Sure it helps," answered Judy. I know I'll see my mother again in heaven. But being a Christian doesn't take away all pain. I have Jesus to help see me through even these hard times."

Hearing those words was a turning point for Diane. She had assumed Christians never experienced grief. Sharing that moment of sorrow demonstrated that Christians are not isolated from reality. Diane could identify with that.

(Adapted from *The Master's Plan* by Win Arn and Charles Arn. Copyright © 1982 by Church Growth Press. Used by permission.)

Think about people who have shared God's love in concrete ways with you—a Sunday school teacher who encouraged you, a pastor who came to your hospital bed, a parent who sacrificed so you could buy the boots you had your heart set on, the forgiveness and understanding of a loving spouse, a friend who listened while you cried. Thank God for them. As you are motivated by God's love for you in Christ Jesus commit to share your love and in so doing His love for others.

Jesus, as always, has done it first.

> As the Father has loved Me, so have I loved you. Now remain in My love. If you obey My commands, you will remain in My love, just as I have obeyed My Father's commands and remain in His love. ... My command is this: Love each other as I have loved you. Greater love has no one than this, that he lay down his life for his friends. You are My friends if you do what I command. ... You did not choose Me, but I chose you and appointed you to bear much fruit—fruit that will last. Then the Father will give you whatever you ask in My name. This is My commandment: Love each other. (John 15:9–17)

Christ's love motivates us to commit our time, emotion, and possessions—our very lives—to the care of others. Through your loving friendships, you are "bearing fruit that will last" through all eternity. It is well worth the investment.

To Consider and Discuss

1. Who is the first known member of your family to have been a Christian? Make a "web" of your family and how God used relationships within it to spread His Word.

2. Take an informal survey of the people in this class. Do the percentages of ways people came into the church match the statistics given in this session? What does this fact mean to your congregation in terms of time and budget?

3. Do you agree that new Christians are best at sharing their faith with others? Why or why not?

4. Tell about a time you comforted someone who was grieving. What did you say? What did you do? How did the person react?

5. Which of the following makes cultivating relationships difficult for you?
   Lack of time
   Do not see the need
   Cannot find anyone to develop a relationship with

Fear of speaking about religion

Other _____

Find a partner in your class and discuss these difficulties. Pray for each other.

6. Analyze the words and actions of the men in the two scenarios dramatized in this session. What made one effective and the other ineffective?

7. Write one act of care you will demonstrate this week with/for your friend.

8. What caused Jesus to lay down His life for not only His friends, but also His enemies? What motivates you to be a friend to others?

9. How can doing "all for the glory of God," as Paul encourages, help lead people to Christ?

10. What could your congregation do to support you in this work? To energize you? To assist you?

Session 4
Tell Me

About This "God Stuff"

The nervous parent, four-year-old daughter in tow, approached the director at a Christian early childhood center. Running a few steps ahead was her noisy two-year-old. In the middle of all the activity and confusion, the director answered the mother's typical questions regarding class size, curriculum, and tuition. Then the mother, of Jewish heritage but inactive in any religious affiliation, fell awkwardly silent. The director waited, knowing a question was being formed. They watched the children play for long minutes. Finally the woman spoke. "So," she said with a sigh, "tell me about this God stuff"?

What would her children be taught at such a school, she wondered. Would it cause trouble in her family? Would her children bring home questions she would not be able to answer? "Tell me." Her question was obvious. How would you answer, in 25 words or less (okay, make it 50 words), with distractions all around you, in words a non-Christian could understand? Try it now. What about this "God stuff"? Who is He and what does He have to do with you? And with her?

That was difficult, wasn't it? Why? Maybe because there is just *so much* to tell. How do you know where to begin? Maybe because your faith in God is a very personal issue, you are uncomfortable sharing those most intimate feelings. Maybe because you don't really know the answer, you've never thought of it in those terms before. Maybe because you are afraid you will say the wrong thing and alienate a person.

If you have cultivated the friendships encouraged in the previous sessions, sooner or later, you will be asked, in one form or another, the same question:

Tell me!

Why do you take me to lunch when you could be eating with the boss?

What happens at that church of yours that makes you go every-Sunday?

How can you keep from giving up when you know you are deathly ill?

What is it you read in that well-worn Bible I see on your end table?

You went to church *how* many times over the Christmas holidays?

How many times are you going to forgive him?

What do you believe about life after death?

I'm so scared/hurt/sad.

Tell me!

1 Peter 3:15 urges: "But in your hearts set apart Christ as Lord. Always be prepared to give an answer to everyone who asks you to give the reason for the hope that you have. But do this with gentleness and respect."

If you are going to deal with those hard questions, says Peter, first be sure the answer is already recorded deep within you. You can't tell what you don't already know. You can't share what you don't already have. Is Christ Lord of your life? You will know it if He is. You will see Him fitting securely in a cross-shaped niche. You will remember becoming His child by the power of the Holy Spirit working through the Gospel—spoken or visible in Holy Baptism. You will hear Him speaking forgiveness and hope daily to you through His Word. You will recall the times He has delivered you just as He promised. You will find yourself spending time with Him in prayer. You will be looking at yourself and others through His eyes of acceptance and love, and you will be looking ahead to an eternity with Him in heaven. By the power of the Holy Spirit, you believe the clear words of Scripture, "I have called you by name, you are Mine" (Isaiah 43:1 RSV) and "By grace you have been saved, through faith" (Ephesians 2:8).

If you cannot yet make that claim, stop here. Develop a friendship with a Christian brother or sister who can lead you into a closer relationship with your Savior. Or continue to study God's Word. God promises that by the power of the Holy Spirit working through His Word He will strengthen your faith. God will prepare you to tell others what it means to have a relationship with Him through Christ, the Lord of your life.

Peter says to be ready to give an answer to everyone who asks you about the reason for your hope. If you were going to participate in a debate, you would prepare by doing research, organizing your thoughts, writing down ideas so you wouldn't forget, and perhaps even practicing in a "trial" match. If you were going to perform in a piano recital, you would prepare by playing your piece of music over and over again until it became second nature to you. When the recital day finally arrived and you sat down on the bench, the music would flow effortlessly and expressively through your well-rehearsed fingers. Do you remember learning to drive a car? Your first excursions were white-knucklers as you grasped the steering wheel and made your way hesitantly through the traffic. Now you feel like the car is an extension of yourself. You automatically operate it with precision and expertise.

Why should telling people about your relationship with God be any different? It will seem awkward until you get used to doing it. It is true, the Holy Spirit motivates and directs us and gives us the words to say. But master craftsmen do their best work when using finely honed tools. For your own piece of mind, *prepare* what you want to express. Be the best tool you can be in the hands of the Master.

Here are a few guidelines to keep in mind:

1. Keep it simple. What do we need to know for salvation? There are three basic understandings:

- People need a Savior. Sin infects the world and everyone in it. Those who suffer have no trouble believing this truth. Life is not fair. People hurt. We do things we do not want to do and cannot do what we should. We need to be rescued.

- Jesus is our Savior who rescued us from sin, death, and the power of Satan. The Bible tells us that by His death on the cross Jesus has paid the punishment for the sins of the world and restored our sin-broken relationship with God. As true God, His life and death count for us. We are free.
- As God's saved people, we live under the care and direction of a God who loves us. In response to His love we are empowered to live according to His will and demonstrate His love and forgiveness to others.

People have expressed these three truths in countless ways. C. F. W. Walther, first president of The Lutheran Church—Missouri Synod, stated that every Christian ought to be able to tell the following:

- How much I needed Christ
- How much Christ did for me
- How I came to faith in Him

A ten-year-old student told his friend:

- "I messed up."
- "Jesus forgives me."
- "I just want to thank Him."

A four-year-old child told her teacher:

- "Jesus loves me even when I'm bad."
- "I told Mandy, 'I forgive you.' That's what Jesus does."

That preschool director told the woman in the beginning of this chapter: "We teach the children that God loves us and takes care of us. Jesus is our Savior. He forgives us, and we forgive each other."

The explanation to the Small Catechism puts it this way (question 85):

- "The Law teaches us what we are to do and not to do ... [it] shows us our sin."
- "The Gospel teaches what God has done, and still does, for our salvation. ... The Gospel shows us our Savior and the grace of God."
- "The Gospel is the means by which the Holy Spirit offers us all the blessings of Christ and creates faith in us" (question 161).

Scripture says,

- "The wages of sin is death" (Romans 6:23).
- "the gift of God is eternal life in Christ Jesus our Lord" (Romans 6:23).

- "If any man is in Christ, he is a new creation" (2 Corinthians 5:17).

2. Tell *your* story. What has Christ done for *you?* How? When? Why? How do you know? How does it make you feel?

3. Use real words. Chances are the people you tell will not know the meanings of "church talk." How can you explain these basic concepts in terms your friend will understand? Think of a picture or example to illustrate each of them. Some examples are listed, but try, also, to come up with some of your own. Try to be specific and relevant to the person you are telling.

Sin. Sin is separation between you and God, which results in separation between you and other people. Think of a space between two tall cliffs. You try to jump across the gap, but it is impossible to do so. No matter how close you come, if you do not make it to the other side, you fall and die. You cannot bridge the gap by yourself.

Redemption. You pawn your watch to get money to pay the light bill. Your friend pays the pawn ticket so you can get your watch back. Satan controlled us until Jesus paid the price to reclaim us for God again.

Sanctification. It means to make holy. If you find an old but valuable coin and bring it home, you clean it and polish it so it will be useful and bring recognition to you. When God claims us as His own, He cleans our lives and uses us to serve Him. This isn't something we choose to do for ourselves. The power and motivation come from the Holy Spirit at work in us.

Faith. Faith means more than just hoping for the best or agreeing intellectually that the facts of the Bible are true. It means putting your whole trust in the fact that God is dependable. It is surrendering your life into God's hands. The Holy Spirit must create this faith in us.

Eternal life. Life in heaven does not mean becoming an angel and floating around on a cloud forever. It is knowing that you will exist in total happiness, enjoying an intimate relationship with God. Think of a book or movie that you liked so much you hated to have it end. Think of a relationship you wanted to go on and on and to never change.

Salvation. The picture of rescuing a person who is drowning is a vivid one. That person cannot help himself. I am told a drowning victim's instinct is to thrash about in the water, trying to save himself, but such efforts only make rescue more difficult. In order to be saved, the victim must remain totally in the rescuer's control. Our efforts to save ourselves are not only futile, they get in the way of our accepting Jesus' full and compete salvation.

God's judgment. Everyone would like to think of God as a benevolent grandfather who overlooks the foibles of His people. The Bible is clear that God is a God of justice. His holiness will not tolerate sin of any kind. He is like a judge who must live by and uphold the law even when a friend stands before Him. That is why Jesus had to die to satisfy the penalties the law required. He paid the fine imposed upon us. Justice has been served.

Worship. Worship is God speaking to us and, in response to His love, we speak to Him. It involves thanks and praise. It involves a recognition of the price He has paid to make us His own. We would not be worthy to worship God if Jesus had not made us clean from sin. At camp, before every meal, the campers are required to pass by the nurse for a dirty hand inspection. Only those whose hands are clean are permitted inside to eat. In the same way God accepts the worship only of those whom He has forgiven through the sacrifice of Jesus, His Son. Jesus holds His nail-pierced hands before the Father as we pass by.

Scripture. This is another word for the Bible. The Bible contains God's word and God's truth and God's promise. Its central theme is God working to save people from their sin. The Old Testament, written before the time Jesus lived on this earth, tells the story of the people of Israel and how God delivered and preserved them in spite of their willful disobedience. It points to Jesus and foretells His coming. There are many passages in the Old Testament that tell about specific things Jesus would say or do. The New Testament was written after Jesus lived on this earth. It tells of His life, death, and resurrection. It shows how He saved all people from sin. Other parts of the New Testament tell about the early church, expand on the truths about the person and work of Jesus, and give directives on how God wants His people to live in the world today. The last book of the Bible, Revelation, tells of Christ's victory in the face of evil and encourages Christians to trust him. The Bible is really a collection of 66 individual "books," each written as God directed the authors and, thus, God's true Word. These books were put together into the Bible as we know it by the early Christian church. It is trustworthy and true. It applies to my own life now.

Holy. Holy means perfect—without any flaw. God is holy, and His holiness demands that His people be perfect also. We are unable to be holy, however; Jesus lived a perfect life in our place and then suffered the punishment we deserved because of our sin. Now when God looks at us He sees Jesus' perfect life and gives us credit for it. In His eyes, by His gift of faith, we are holy.

Born again. The Bible says that a person must be "born again" before he can enter into God's family. That means that the power of sin all people are born under must be overcome. It is like having a new start in life. When a child born in poverty is adopted into the family of royalty, that child begins a whole new life in a whole new relationship. We receive God's forgiveness through faith in Jesus. This faith is a gift; we do not decide we want it, just as a baby does not decide to be born or adopted.

Some churches teach that being "born again" is a decision based on reason or emotion. The Bible is clear that our relationship with God is not of our own choosing. We are His own even when we don't feel like it. The *fact* is that He has made us a part of His family just as surely as Jesus died on the cross and rose again.

The new relationship we have been born into is based on what God has done—not on what we do or do not do. We still do wrong things and think wrong thoughts and suffer the consequences of sin. But we live in the ongoing forgiveness of God through Christ, always a part of His family, always connected to His support and love. So our relationship with God through Jesus is constant. God calls us from our sins through His Law, and He provides us His forgiveness through faith in Jesus—the Gospel.

Sacrament. The Holy Spirit works faith in our hearts through the

Gospel—His Good News of forgiveness through Jesus. The Gospel can be read or heard from the Bible or it can be applied in a tangible way according to His plan. Scripture mentions two concrete ways in which God works faith and forgives sins. The first is through

Baptism—"Get up, be baptized, and wash your sins away" (Acts 22:16) in which the medium of water is used. The second is

Holy Communion, or the Lord's Supper—"This is My body. ..."

This is My blood of the covenant which is poured out for many for the forgiveness of sins" (Matthew 26:26–28) in which Christ's body and blood are present in, with, and under the bread and wine.

These tangible expressions of the Gospel connected to God's Word and through which God forgives sins are called sacraments.

Trinity/Triune. Three in one. This concept is a mystery that cannot be totally understood. We believe it because this is how the Bible describes God. Some human illustrations may be helpful. For example, an egg consists of three parts—the shell, the white, and the yolk, but there is only one egg. This example is imperfect, however, because the three components can be separated and can exist independently of each other. Another example commonly used is of a shamrock—with three segments, yet only one leaf. The Bible speaks of God the Father, who created and sustains all things; God the Son, Jesus, who became also true man and lived and died to save us; and God the Holy Spirit, who works through God's Word to create and to strengthen saving faith. Each is a distinct person, each is described by His function; yet the three cannot be divided. When confronted with concepts which we cannot understand with our human wisdom, we must defer to God's superiority.

Fellowship. This is a word that means the close friendship or unity which exists among Christians because of the saving faith they share in Christ Jesus. God's people enjoy each other's company and provide support for each other.

Can you think of other words that may be confusing?

If you are studying this book as a class, divide the class into small groups and assign each group several of the words listed above. Then share with each other the examples you formulated.

4. Keep it short. You may think your experiences rival those of St. Paul, but your listener will be easily overwhelmed. It is better to leave your listener with questions to be answered later than to bore your friend with too much too soon. Your goal is to create a safe and trusting friendship in which it is possible to speak of these things often as you search deeper into the truths of God's plan of redemption.

5. Invite questions and discussion. People do not like to be told what to believe. They need to ask questions and explore possibilities. Do not view their questions as a threat. They are testing to see if what you say holds up. If the discussion turns to bitter argument, stop. Remember, you are merely "telling it." It is the job of the

Holy Spirit to convince and convert. The claims of Scripture stand up to honest inquiry. But the Bible is not a book about science or anthropology. It is the story of God redeeming His people. Keep your focus on what God has done for you and for your friend. Faith is not based on logical arguments. Faith is a gift of God provided by the Holy Spirit working through God's Word.

6. It is helpful to have portions of Scripture memorized to use appropriately. Remember, this is really God's story. A few quotes from the Author adds authenticity and power. Resolve to memorize one pertinent Bible passage each week. You can identify these passages as you read God's Word daily, or books are available which organize passages according to topic. Be careful, however, not to thump your friend over the head with weighty passages that are difficult to understand. Share verses that have been helpful to you personally in your walk of faith.

7. Think GOSPEL. While the Law is necessary to show people their need for a Savior, most people who feel the need to ask about your God are probably already feeling the need for His forgiveness. Their hearts convict them. You do not need to make them feel worse. If you came upon an accident and found a person bleeding to death, you would not stop to lecture that person on the necessity of keeping blood inside the body. You would stop the bleeding. The problem is obvious. It is your job to provide the solution. In the same way if a friend comes to you seeking solutions, show him or her Jesus.

8. Encourage a statement of faith. Suppose your friend is moved to believe in Jesus as you do. Like the jailer in Philippi, she asks, "What must I do to be saved?" Do NOT give her a laundry list which begins, "First, you must ask Jesus into your heart." If she is asking, the Holy Spirit has already entered her heart. It was not her decision. Ask, instead, "Do you believe that Jesus is your Savior from sin and the only way to heaven? Do you confess Him as Lord of your life? Then you *are* a member of God's family. You *have* His salvation." Then plan together ways to nurture that newly born faith and commitment to the Lord.

Start simple. In the space below tell one thing you like about Jesus.

Read your words to someone else in your class or in your congregation. Practice saying the same ideas without reading them. Now do the same with the following questions:

When did you become a Christian? How?

Why do you go to church?

How is your life as a Christian different from what it would be if you were not a Christian?

What do you believe happens when you die?

Picture the friend with whom you have been developing a relationship. What questions do you anticipate that person asking you? Write out an answer to those questions now.

Tell!

John the Baptist, Jesus' cousin and friend, desperately *needed* to know. He had devoted his life to proclaiming the Lordship of Jesus. He had lived in the wilderness, forgoing any comforts or worldly pleasures. He wore scratchy clothes and went without haircuts and ate disgusting foods to make his life an object lesson of the separation sin brings into the world. He renounced his own reputation and spent the prime of his life pointing to Jesus as the promised Messiah. Finally, because of his dedication to proclaim the Word of the Lord he was about to die. He had gone too far. He had spoken words of judgment on King Herod and his relationship with Herod's brother's wife. Now Herod was mad and John the Baptist was about to lose his life as a result of his commitment. He just had to ask one more time. Was it all worth it? Was Jesus really who He said He was, or had it all been some terrible hoax? He sent his trusted disciples with that one essential question: "Are you the one who was to come, or should we expect someone else? *[Tell me!]*" (Matthew 11:2).

Jesus' answer is perfect. "Go back and report to John what you hear and see: The blind receive sight, the lame walk, those who have leprosy are cured, the deaf hear, the dead are raised, and the good news is preached to the poor" (Matthew 11:4–5).

He sends them back to tell what they know, what they have personally seen and experienced.

Jesus gives us the same command. "*Tell them,*" He says, "what you have seen for yourself."

And then what? After you tell, your listener can respond in one of several ways:

1. "Wow! You are right! I never realized it before. I want to be a part of God's family, too."
2. "You've got to be kidding. I could never fall for a story like that."
3. "Let me think about this for a while."
4. "That may be okay for you, but not for me."
5. "What in the world are you talking about?"
6. "Tell me more."
7. "What are you, some kind of a religious nut or something?"

It's a risk, isn't it? Not really. The response, you see, is in God's hands. He asks you only to tell. He may ask someone else to tell again later. He may give you another opportunity at another time. He may take that person home before another day passes. He does make one promise, however. He promises that wherever His Word is proclaimed, it will have an effect. Isaiah 55:10–11 states: "As the rain and the snow come down from heaven, and do not return to it without watering the earth and making it bud and flourish so that it yields seed for the sower and bread for the eater, so is My word that goes out from My mouth. It will not return to Me empty, but will accomplish what I desire and achieve the purpose for which I sent it."

God's Word, as spoken through you, will accomplish what He desires.

Read? Now?

Sharing God's Word with your friends is not something you plan or control. When the opportunity presents itself, you are, however, called upon to be ready. Do you feel ready now?

George Barna, in *Evangelism That Works*, has compiled some interesting statistics.

- 85 percent of those who share the Gospel say they would like to have been better prepared.
- 91 percent say they usually share their faith unexpectedly in the course of normal conversation.
- 40 percent are concerned that they will not do a good job of explaining their beliefs.
- 30 percent worry that the person they are speaking to will be upset or offended by the nature of the discussion.
- 14 percent feel uncomfortable speaking with other people about spiritual matters.

Where do you fit in? If you are sharing your faith with a friend in response to a direct question, some of the fears should be alleviated.

Barna has also studied ways in which people share faith with others.

- 79 percent promote the benefits of being a Christian. This approach appeals to many listeners, who see God as a provider of spiritual gifts.
- 75 percent involve the other person in the process by asking questions about their beliefs and life experiences.
- 59 percent tell the story of how they first came to know Christ as their Savior.
- 58 percent quote passages from the Bible to make their case.
- 54 percent pray before getting together with someone to discuss spiritual truths.

Does it work?

- During the year 1994 more than 60 million adults shared their religious beliefs with another person in the hope of bringing that person to Christ.
- People who share their faith with others do so often—on the average of once a month.
- Although about half of all adults indicate they become

annoyed when someone tries to share religious beliefs with them, when the conversation is with a family member or close friend, they are not annoyed. In fact, they often express gratitude for the interest shown in them.

(From *Evangelism That Works* by George Barna. Copyright © 1995 by Regal Books, Ventura, CA 93003. Used by permission.)

What about your friend? Has your relationship progressed to the point at which you openly share feelings and concerns? Then watch for opportunities to *tell* about the most important part of your life. God has prepared you. He has given you a wonderful story to tell. He will give you opportunities to tell it again and again according to His all-knowing will.

Look back at the paragraph you wrote at the beginning of this session. Read it aloud to yourself and to a friend. Does it say what you want it to say? Revise it if you wish. Practice telling it until it slips through your lips at the slightest provocation. Tell it to yourself in the shower. Tell it to the cat at the end of the day. Tell it to your mother and to your grandchild. Tell it to anyone who asks you to give a reason for the hope that is in you. It is your story. It is God's story about you, ... and Him, ... and your friend.

When you see a friend or relative's name mentioned in the newspaper, your first response is to let that person know. You might even cut the article out and make copies to mail to other friends and relatives. Your friend's name is mentioned in God's book. He would have *all* to be saved. Show him. Tell her. Spread the Word.

Join in the chorus of the familiar old song:

> **Refrain: I love to tell the story;**
> **'Twill be my theme in glory,**
> **To tell the old, old story**
> **Of Jesus and His love.**
>
> **I love to tell the story**
> **Of unseen things above,**
> **Of Jesus and His glory,**
> **Of Jesus and His love.**
> **I love to tell the story,**
> **Because I know 'tis true.**
> **It satisfies my longing**
> **As nothing else can do.**
>
> **I love to tell the story,**
> **For those who know it best**

Seem hungering and thirsting
To hear it like the rest.
And when in scenes of glory
I sing a new, new song,
'Twill be the old, old story
That I have loved so long.

To Consider and Discuss

1. Think of some of the people you have told about Jesus. Have you seen any of the results? Continue praying for these people.

2. What concept about God is difficult for you to explain to your unchurched friends? Ask your pastor or a Christian friend to give you ideas that would help communicate that concept more effectively. How do you talk about those parts of faith and affirm your faith while still acknowledging there is much you don't understand?

3. Who first told you about Jesus? Do you remember the circumstances surrounding the event? Thank that individual, if possible, in person or in a letter.

4. One person relates the three essential components of the Gospel by drawing three faces: A sad face, a happy face, and a "telly" face (a face with the mouth open). How would you elaborate on those pictures to complete the story?

5. Sometimes objects can illustrate the truths of God's Word. What parallels could you draw between concepts about God and the following?
   - An umbrella
   - A life jacket
   - A seed
   - A bottle of medicine
   - A pickle
   - A tree
   - A computer
   - Other_____
   - Other_____

6. Some people find it easier to talk about their faith to children rather than adults. Volunteer to help in a Sunday school class to practice telling about God's love. Do you find children receptive to your story? Why did Jesus say everyone who enters into His kingdom must become like a little child? What is the difference between being "childish" and "childlike" in your faith?

7. Think about the people you are befriending. Write here the name of the first person you plan to tell the story of God's work in your life and the circumstances you foresee leading up to it. Ask another Christian friend to pray for you; pray for that person also.

8. Find a passage in Scripture that will encourage you when you begin to share your faith. Write it here.

9. After you have told someone about your relationship with Christ, record that person's response in the space below. Analyze the response and plan your next conversation.

Session 5 Gathering Two or Three

"I can do it myself!" What parents have not heard their toddler loudly make that declaration of independence? God heard it first in the Garden, when Eve took matters into her own hands and chose to make her own decisions based on her own desires rather than on God's will for her.

In leading friends to Christ, we, too, are tempted to want to do it on our own. We have identified the friend; we have cultivated the friendship; we have prayed and shared our personal testimony. We have put ourselves and our relationship at risk and are finally sensing victory.

Now we feel strong ownership of this relationship. We want to bring it to completion and lead our friend hand in hand to the heavenly gates.

The good news is this: we are not in this by ourselves.

No one can be everything to everyone.

Even the greatest football player needs the skills of his team in order to make touchdowns. The smartest scientist builds on the wisdom of those who have gone before. The most competent surgeon works with assistants.

Look first at Jesus. With an entire world to win, He chose not to go it alone. He enlisted the help of twelve disciples—His support group; His ministry team; His prayer partners; His proteges. As true Man, He experienced all the limitations of real men. When He grew tired, someone had to row the boat. When He needed a ride, someone had to fetch a donkey. After hosting 5,000 people for dinner, He became tired. Jesus worked together with others in order to accomplish His purposes.

Who can help you lead your friend to Jesus? Once you have established a relationship with an individual, you will want to introduce that person to other Christians. This multiplies your effectiveness and will provide additional support for the new Christian.

Research indicates that unchurched and "dechurched" people today are not particularly interested in spiritual matters: 91 percent indicate their primary concern is about their own health; 74 percent are seeking close, personal friendships; 71 percent strive to maintain a comfortable lifestyle; 71 percent also search for a clear purpose for living. Only 15 percent believe that being a part of a local church is important. (*Barna*, p. 57)

What do these statistics say to you, one who is seeking to bring your friend into the fellowship of God's people? They say not to expect an enthusiastic reaction to words such as, "You really ought to visit our church. Our pastor preaches terrific sermons!" This is not to say you should never invite your friend to church. It just may not be the most effective first step.

Instead, use those natural interests and needs to introduce more Christian friends into the relationship. If health is a concern, get together a walking group or join a health club where other Christians are members. Do you have friends who backpack or hike? Do you know people in Weight Watchers? Every Christian community includes a variety of personalities with a variety of interests. Introduce your unchurched friend to other Christians with similar concerns and involvements.

Parents recognize an immediate common bond with other parents in similar circumstances. Consider play groups, co-op baby-sitting, or car-pooling to school or practices. Invite a group to attend a lecture or class together. Some of these activities may even take place at your church, but the emphasis is on involving your friend in enjoyable, productive pursuits that focus on his or her needs in the company of other Christians.

In a society where people move easily from city to city and state to state, where young families are often separated from extended family and childhood friends, people seek a sense of belonging. They feel strong loyalty to a group who will include them and value them. Athletic teams, handicraft clubs, historical societies, and service groups all provide camaraderie, security, and support. When these groups consist of fellow Christians, they can provide a link between that person and the church and between that person and his perception of God. Many unchurched people believe that church members are somber, critical do-nothings. They are pleasantly surprised to find that Christians are people just like themselves, with interests and talents and a sense of humor. They are drawn into the fellowship as friends, not as prospective members of a church.

Another gap which modern-day human beings seek to fill is the need to do something worthwhile with their lives—to be a part of something beyond themselves—to help people who need to be helped. The motivation for this altruistic urge may involve a sense of guilt at having so much while others have so little. Or it may be a genuine inborn concern for others. Most people feel good doing something good for society. In this area the church has countless opportunities to channel those needs toward worthwhile causes. Working together with Christian people to collect food for the homeless or build an orphanage across the border or take meals to shut-ins or even run a refreshment booth for the community fair forms close bonds between participants.

Sometimes people get together just for the fun of it. Be sure your unchurched friend knows your spouse and family. Share a meal or a movie or a holiday celebration at which other Christians will be present.

What happens when people are included with groups of Christians? The ministry is multiplied. If possible, let your Christian friends know ahead of time that you are concentrating on this particular individual. Enlist prayer support. Share any particular facts that would prove helpful without betraying any confidences. For example, you might mention that your friend has recently lost his job. Knowing this fact alerts others not to put him in an awkward situation such as being expected to order an expensive meal. It also opens the way for networking a solution to the problem. Perhaps someone in the group can provide a lead for a job. Be sure that the information you share is common knowledge and would not embarrass your friend in any way. Usually, once people feel accepted in a group, they will share information and feelings freely in that setting.

There are two aspects involved in introducing your friend to fellow Christians. The first is that your friend be made to feel welcome. The initial meeting must be cordial and nonthreatening. Be sure everyone knows each other's name and a bit of information that will help make that person identifiable. This is Bill; he is a carpenter, and he builds custom homes. Mary has a daughter the same age as Jennifer. They are in the same Brownie troop. Don't overdo it. Give the newcomer time to observe and feel comfortable. Think about how you feel when meeting someone new. You want to feel included, but you also need space to make your own decisions about intimacy. Be sure the Christian friends you are enlisting are open to including others.

The second aspect of being a part of a group is acceptance. Once you are no longer a "visitor," when everyone was on their best behavior, now what? It is important that people feel they are valued and appreciated—that their company is enjoyed. If your friend joins the softball team, he needs to play a position on the field, not sit on the bench. If everyone goes out after the game, he needs to be invited along. If you spend an afternoon shopping, your friend needs to ride with you and be let in on the "in group" jokes. She needs to be called about what to wear and included in the planning for the next get-together.

All of these interactions are informal. You are widening the circle of Christian influence on your unchurched friend. They are genuine outgrowths of friendship, not a pyramid scheme designed to brainwash or entrap. They provide support for you, the Gospel-sharer, and open new avenues of caring for your friend.

It may be possible to include your unchurched friend in large groups of fellow Christians. Often, however, you may want to introduce only one. That was the case with the servant girl mentioned in 2 Kings 5.

We are not even told her name, but she is a prime example of identifying a person in need and introducing that person to her God. She was captured by the Arameans and, as was the custom, made to serve in the household of her conqueror. It was not exactly a relationship of her choosing, but it was the situation in which she found herself, so she made the best of it, and God used her in an amazing way. When her master, Naaman, became ill with leprosy she knew there was only one source of help. Her God could provide the cure. But this girl was in no position to make such a suggestion directly. First she enlisted the help of her mistress, Naaman's wife. "Tell your husband to see the prophet of God in Samaria," she urged.

Naaman's wife convinced him to give it a try, and the king of Aram gave him permission to go. So Naaman set out with a letter of reference from his king to the king of Israel on the word of an insignificant servant girl. The king of Israel was no help. He didn't see the big picture. Instead of welcoming this "seeker," he was about to send him away. The prophet Elisha heard about the situation and stepped in with an invitation. "Come on over," he offered, "and I'll show you what a prophet of God can do." And he did. Naaman was cured of his leprosy and, as a result, confessed, "Now I know that there is no God in all the world except in Israel." (2 Kings 5:15) He acknowledged Elisha's God, the God of his servant girl, to be Lord of all.

Do you know someone with whom you are unable to communicate effectively? Introduce that person to a friend, a colleague, another "prophet" who can meet that person's need more directly. Perhaps your role in that particular relationship is to be a "scout." You have identified the unchurched person and passed that person on to another circle of care. Being able to identify and match up caregivers with those who need them is a gift. If you are a person who comes into contact with many people and who knows rich networks of individuals and groups, allow God to use you in this way.

List in this space the names of fellow Christians who are specialized "resource" people with whom you might connect a person with a particular need.

Moses was another person who knew how to enlist the support of others. God had placed him in a position of familiarity and influence. He had access to Pharaoh and his court; he had acceptance among the Israelite people. Moses may not have been Pharaoh's "friend," but he certainly had connections. Yet when it came time to proclaim God's specific words to Pharaoh and the Israelites, the feet God had warmed in the glow of the Burning Bush turned cold. Moses remembered he had a speech deficiency. Then he uttered the most common prayer of all those God drafts into His service, "O Lord, please send somebody else!" That "somebody else" turned out to be Moses' brother, Aaron. God enhanced Moses' ministry by teaming him with a cohort. He even gave Moses the strategy, "You shall speak to him [Aaron] and put words in his mouth; I will help both of you speak and will teach you what to do. He will speak to the people for you, and it will be as if he were your mouth and as if you were God to him" (Exodus 4:15–17).

Do you have a close Christian cohort—a partner who complements your own gifts and abilities—a Tonto to your Lone Ranger—a Robin to your Batman—a Tweedledee to your Tweedledum? Work together. Strategize. Pray for each other. Seek each other when things get tense. Volunteer yourselves for God's service so that He will "help both of you to speak and will teach you what to do."

In the space below list at least three fellow Christians to whom you feel close. Behind their names, write their strengths. Think about ways you could team with them to accomplish a particular task.

Philip never even knew what hit him. He was minding his own business—well, actually, the Lord's business—probably in Jerusalem where he and his fellow deacons had started out dealing with disputes among widows and organizing potluck suppers, when God enlisted him for service. "Your assignment, if you should choose to accept it (which you will, of course), is to head south. Just start walking. You'll know when you get there." That's how Philip found himself in the middle of a dusty desert road in the middle of nowhere. Along came a chariot, gaining on Philip, heading toward Ethiopia. Philip's first instinct must have been to get out of the way. Let the vehicle pass; avoid being run over. Keep walking. Then a strange thing happened. Philip felt the need to run after the chariot and keep up with it. When he got closer, he heard the passenger reading some familiar words from the book of Isaiah, "He was led like a sheep to the slaughter, and as a lamb before the shearer is silent, so he opened not his mouth" (Acts 8:32).

"Do you understand all that?" asked Philip. *"Tell me,"* pleaded the Ethiopian. And Philip knew just what to say. As a result, the man came to know Jesus as the Lamb of God who died for him, and he was baptized right there along the side of the road. Then, BAM! The Bible says Philip was suddenly taken away. His mission at that place was accomplished. It was back to other roads God had in mind.

Have you ever wondered why an Ethiopian was reading the book of Isaiah in the first place? Notice where he had been. He was coming from Jerusalem, where he had worshiped at the temple. A Gentile convert, he had received some knowledge about the Lord, but he didn't know it all. Someone else had laid the groundwork.

Someone else had provided him a copy of the scroll. Someone else had piqued his interest. Now it was Philip's turn to lead this man's understanding to the next step.

Where do you fit into the picture of your unchurched friend's life? Are you the first to make contact? Have others gone before you, laying cable to which you can now connect? Do you feel frustrated that you cannot see the end of the story because your link with your friend is suddenly changed or broken? Stand in the road with Philip and snag the chariots that the Lord sends your way. Know that you are not the first or last person God will bring into any person's life. Keep busy in the place where God has put you; He will know where to find you when He seeks your service.

In the space below list the names of people you know will be a part of your life for only a short while. Plan a time to cross paths with them in a setting that is conducive to conversation. Make a connection. Be open to their needs. Be ready to build on someone else's foundation or begin laying one on which others can build.

St. Paul was a master at enlisting the troops in the process of proclaiming the Gospel. Watch God in action through Paul at Corinth. As you read, underline the names of the people Paul involved in his ministry.

> After this, Paul ... went to Corinth. There he met a Jew named Aquila, a native of Pontus, who had recently come from Italy with his wife, Priscilla, because Claudius had ordered all the Jews to leave Rome. Paul went to see them, and because he was a tentmaker as they were, he stayed and worked with them. Every Sabbath he reasoned in the synagogue, trying to persuade Jews and Greeks. When Silas and Timothy came from Macedonia, Paul devoted himself exclusively to preaching, testifying to the Jews that Jesus was the Christ. ...

> Then Paul left the synagogue and went next door to the house of Titius Justus, a worshiper of God. Crispus, the synagogue ruler, and his entire household believed in the Lord; and many of the Corinthians who heard him believed and were baptized. ...

One night the Lord spoke to Paul in a vision: "Do not be afraid; keep on speaking, do not be silent. For I am with you, and no one is going to attack and harm you. I have many people in this city." (Acts 18: 1-11)

How did each of these support Paul's ministry?
Aquila

Priscilla

Silas

Timothy

Titius Justus

Crispus

God's "many people" in the city

Each of these individuals carried on one part of the Lord's work. Paul had learned from experience that God provides the people He needs to accomplish His will. Can you recall a time when support was there just when you needed it? Have you ever been the "relief" person for someone else?

Jesus' promise rings in our ears: "If two of you on earth agree about anything you ask for, it will be done for you by my Father in heaven. For where two or three come together in my name, there am I with them" (Matthew 18:19–20).

There is power in combined care and concern. While one strand of a rope may be easily broken, many strands intertwined create a network that will hold even under the greatest pressure. Paul's words in 2 Corinthians 5:20 underscore the impact made by many people doing God's work together. "*We* are therefore Christ's *ambassadors*, as though God were making His appeal through *us*" (emphasis added).

Becky and Scott moved next door to Myrna and Ray. They became friendly and enjoyed each other's company for bar-b-ques and backyard conversation. When Myrna found out Becky was a quilter, she invited her to the quilting group at church. The group welcomed Becky warmly, and she chatted while she worked along-side Theresa, a widow with two young children. Theresa offered to take Becky along the next time she planned a trip to a discount mall where she could buy fabric remnants at a good price. Myrna rode along, too, and the three had a chance to talk about many things in the car and at lunch. They laughed easily and got some great bargains. "It must be hard," Becky commented, "to raise your children without their father. Life just isn't fair!"

Theresa agreed that she experienced many moments of frustration and sadness, but that she knew her husband was in heaven and that God continued to provide for her each day. While Theresa was talking, Myrna was busy praying that God would give Theresa the right words to say and that Becky's heart would be receptive to the Gospel message she was hearing.

The subject then changed to other topics. But the three friends found themselves together often, and when Becky expressed an interest, both Myrna and Theresa spoke openly about God and His work in their lives.

When Myrna was suddenly hospitalized with acute appendicitis, Becky called Theresa to let her know. "I suppose we should pray for her," she suggested. "Would you show me how?"

"Let's pray together," responded Theresa, and they did. They visited Myrna at the hospital and prayed for her there, too. Becky knew that her friends were praying for her.

Can you see how God is using Myrna and Theresa to support each other and open avenues of communication with Becky? When Becky meets Myrna's pastor at the hospital, she will feel comfortable with him. When Myrna invites Becky and Scott to attend church with her family in a few weeks, they will be likely to accept. Theresa will be there, too, and will introduce Scott to her brother, an avid fisherman. Scott always did like to fish …

No one person, other than Jesus Christ, has ever been a perfect example of the Christian life. If you are the only Christian your unchurched friend ever has contact with, that person will get a limited view of the church. People need to see an honest representation of what the church is—a collection of people who have been redeemed by their Lord—each being unique and each accepted and loved as a unique person.

Statistics indicate that most people who become active church members had heard the Gospel presented to them an average of 5.8 different times and often by different people before they came to faith in the Lord. People who joined a church but later became inactive had heard the Gospel an average of only twice before deciding to join.

The more Christians people know, the more opportunities there are for them to hear the Gospel presented in meaningful and personal ways.

Did you know that people learn differently? Some are auditory learners. They remember what they have been told. Others are visual learners. They must see what they are to remember. They learn by reading or seeing an example. Still others rely on tactile learning. They must feel or experience the thing they are attempting to learn.

Think about how you learned to program your VCR. Did you call the hot line and follow verbal directions, or did you ask the clerk at the store when you made your purchase? Did you read the instruction book thoroughly and follow the diagrams, or did you go to a friend's house and say, "Show me how you did it. Let me try it on yours"? Or, perhaps, did you just start pushing buttons and connecting cables by trial and error until it worked (or was hopelessly broken, at which time you called the repairman or your 10-year-old daughter)?

Do you know the learning style of your unchurched friend? Is it the same as yours? If you are a "just tell me about it" kind of person and your friend needs to experience things for herself, you may become frustrated when your clear explanations have no effect. Engage the help of another Christian to help her understand.

In addition, we are told that young people today do not learn in the same way as older people. Most people over the age of 30 process information in a linear way. If *A* is true, then it makes sense to proceed to *B*, which leads to the conclusion of *C*. Individuals born after 1970 have grown up in an environment of computers and video games that forces them to deal with a bombardment of stimuli and information. They take in vast amounts of data and process it simultaneously. Are you able to present the Gospel in a nonlinear way to people who are not impressed with inductive reasoning? Are you able to train yourself in new ways of thinking? Are you familiar with resource materials and resource people who are comfortable with fast-paced technology?

Can Baby Boomers share the Gospel effectively with Busters, or should each generation stay within the confines of its own age bracket? Can rich share with poor or Jews with Samaritans? You know Jesus' answer to that one.

Look at the people He touched: children, adults, the aged; sick and well, alive and even dead; Jews, Samaritans, Romans, Greeks; fishermen and tax collectors; distinguished members of the Sanhedrin and common thieves; you—and me. What did they all have in common? He responded to their need for Him. Can you relate to the needs and interests of your friend? Have you established a relationship of caring and trust? Then chances are, you will be able to tell the Gospel message in terms that person can understand.

Are you puzzled by your unchurched friend's attitude? Are you sending but no one is receiving? Do you truly find it hard to relate to that person's situation? Do you *want* to help but honestly don't see which direction to take? Then it is time to pass the baton. Continue to befriend and support your friend, but expand your circle of influence.

Recognizing the need for assistance is the first step toward extending your reach. Get help from wherever you can, from whomever you need. The goal is to communicate God's love to people who do not speak the Gospel language. Find an interpreter and support the translation in every way possible.

Enlisting the help of fellow Christians also provides us with the needed benefit of accountability. Meet regularly with a Christian friend to assess progress and share resources. Again, be careful to respect the confidentiality of your unchurched friend, but ask for your colleague's advice and prayers. If you are getting tired of making friendly overtures with no response, receive encouragement to keep on trying. When you have neglected to follow up on a contact or forgotten to make a call, receive words of assurance and forgiveness. When you see doors opening and progress made, praise God together. Just knowing that you will have the attention and support of another Christian brother or sister keeps you renewed and on task. The importance of praying together cannot be emphasized enough. Trust Jesus' promise of His presence between the two of you, and act on it.

Who Are Your Christian Friends?

Perhaps one more facet needs to be considered. What do we mean by "Christian friends"? Who are these people who are going to multiply your effectiveness as a friend to the unchurched?

Let's begin by identifying who they are *not*. Christian friends are not

- sanctimonious holier-than-thous who draw attention to themselves as moral superiors or lofty examples. Such people are intimidating to non-Christians, who see through the hypocrisy and feel no motivation to get better acquainted. Besides, they are no fun.

> For by the grace given me I say to every one of you: Do not think of yourself more highly than you ought, but rather think of yourself with sober judgment, in accordance with the measure of faith God has given you. (Romans 12:3)

- blatant backsliders who openly and intentionally live a lifestyle that mocks God's commandments. People who live no differently from non-Christians model no alternatives to the unchurched. Why bother? They are just like all the others.

> "You are the light of the world. A city on a hill cannot be hidden. Neither do people light a lamp and put it under a bowl. Instead they put it on its stand and it gives light to everyone in the house. In the same way, let your light shine before men, that they may see your good deeds and praise your Father in heaven." (Matthew 5:14-16)

- doubters of their own salvation. The unchurched are seeking a confident witness to the power of the Gospel. All Christians experience moments of weakness, but those who witness to their faith need to *know* the one in whom they believe, not be drawn into hopeless discussions of mutual despair.

> Be wise in the way you act toward outsiders; make the most of every opportunity. Let your conversation be always full of grace, seasoned with salt, so that you may know how to answer everyone. (Colossians 4:5-6)

Christian friends, then, are
- sinful human beings who have been redeemed by the death of Jesus, their Savior.
- people who live by the grace of God in the power He provides.
- people who experience problems and difficulties in life, but depend upon God to support and help them.
- active members in a Christian church, who pray regularly for themselves and others.

The lives of Christian friends reflect their beliefs, and when they fail, knowing they are forgiven, they go on with strength and motivation renewed by the power of the Holy Spirit working through God's Word to continue striving. They are driven by their love for God to love other people and demonstrate their care. They are willing to sacrifice their own needs and comfort to help others and bring them into the circle of God's family.

Can you think of any other characteristics of Christian friends? List them here:

By definition, are *you* a Christian friend who can be enlisted to assist others in their ministry? The answer is yes, by the grace of God. Thank God that He has given us each other at just the right time and in just the right place.

Ed invited Ron to join the church-league softball team. Ron enjoyed the camaraderie of the other players and loved playing the game. He met Todd, who worked in computer programming like he did, and Howard, who was divorced, just like himself and was dealing with visitation issues. Ron never really thought about the fact that most of his teammates belonged to the same church. They were just good guys who played a good game. He liked the fact that most were nonsmokers. Breathing that junk bothered him, as it must bother the others. Howard offered to go with him to a court date regarding custody rights. Howard was a stand-up guy. Ed couldn't remember the last time someone offered to go out of his way for him like that. Come to think of it, the whole team was great. Oh, sure, Wally was always losing his temper and giving the umpire a bad time. But, all in all, he was glad Ed had included him. He wondered how Howard dealt with his kids' questions about why he didn't live with them any more. He thought he might take Howard up on his offer, after all. He'd like to talk with him about some other things, too. Joining this team was the best thing that had happened to him in a long time. He even liked the prayer that the guys said before each game. He hadn't thought about God for a long time, either, but, for some reason, he wanted to know more.

Wouldn't you like to eavesdrop on the conversation that takes place between Howard and Ron on the way to and from the courtroom?

What would you say if you were Howard?

The U.S. Army urges recruits to "Be all that you can be." In the same way God empowers us to be all that He has made us—for Him and for each other.

To Consider and Discuss

1. Are you the type of person who likes to "do it by myself"? Why? What makes you reluctant to include other Christians in your commitment to share Christ with your friends?

2. How do your concerns compare to the concerns listed in the statistics in this session? Are you most concerned with your health, your lifestyle, and being a part of something meaningful? Do you agree that those are the main considerations of people you know? If not, what are?

3. Are you a fun person to be around? Why or why not?

Think of some ways you could "lighten up" to put less stress on those around you.

4. Think of the groups of Christians with whom you are affiliated. Are they open to newcomers? In what specific ways do they make newcomers feel welcome and accepted? What could they do better?

5. Have you, like Moses, ever prayed, "Here am I. Send him!"? Why? In what areas would you be eager to volunteer?

6. What kind of learner are you? Are you able to communicate with people who are different in age or background? What bridges the gaps? With whom is it very difficult for you to communicate? Who among your Christian friends could communicate with those people?

7. How many times did you hear the Gospel before the Holy Spirit worked faith in your heart? If you were an adult or older child, do you remember what finally made "sense"? If you were baptized as an infant, how can you relate to those who are adults and still not a part of God's family? How would you describe your journey of faith to your unchurched friend?

8. What makes you a Christian friend? What can you do because you are one?

9. Pray now for your unchurched friend and for your fellow Christians. Thank God for bringing them into your life and for bringing you into theirs. Ask for guidance in the days to come, and praise God for His wonderfully diverse family, of which you are a part.

Session 6 Welcome to the Family

On a New Planet?

Imagine you are on the first manned spaceship to the planet Iglesia. You have prepared for this flight by studying all the literature available, and you have met an actual inhabitant of this planet during her recent brief visit to earth. She seemed friendly enough; her language was understandable, and she seemed to like you. But, still, you wonder. When she invited you aboard her spaceship and promised to accompany you all along the way you were excited and eager. But was it only a trick to lure you closer? If everyone on the planet is as agreeable as she is, this will be the adventure of a lifetime. But, if you have been misled, you are truly at risk. You are willing to take the chance. You land on the unfamiliar soil and try to get your bearings.

Who are these people? They are approaching me with—are those smiles or leers? It's okay; they're giving me a map. It seems to correspond to what is happening in the reception center. Where's Iglesiette, my friend? She promised to meet me here. If she were here I wouldn't feel so vulnerable.

At least they do shake hands here. That helps. I think I recognize that guy from my gym back on earth. Oh, yeah, I remember now, he did tell me he had come from here. He sees me. He's coming over. It feels good to see a familiar face.

I guess I'd better sit down for the indoctrination. Where is Iglesiette, anyway? She said she'd be here.

Nice music. It seems to fit the words. I like it. That man sitting at the end of this bench smiled at me, too. I wonder why they don't put in some comfortable seating. Ah, there she is. Hi, Iglesiette. I'm here. So far, so good. Am I dressed okay? I haven't owned a suit since the senior banquet. I think I look like everyone else. Except the master of ceremonies, of course. There must be some reason he's wearing the Yoda outfit. He seems to be set apart for some reason. Oh, no! They're welcoming newcomers. If they slap a ribbon or name tag on me I'm back on the ship. I don't want to stand out. I just want to watch what's going on. I do appreciate the fact that they're glad I'm here. I'd like to meet some more of the natives later. They look a lot like me. That guy in the purple shirt is hugging his wife. Cute. His kids are acting up just like mine would if I ever brought them here, but no one seems to be glaring. I guess this is a safe place for earth people.

More music. A little heavier this time, but not bad. It makes me feel like something important is happening. The words are printed in this "map." If I could figure out the melody, I'd sing along. If I come back another time, maybe we'll sing it again.

"Yoda" is reading now. It's from the Bible. Iglesiette quoted some sections to me before. It's what convinced me to come. I was hoping I would hear more. Yes, it's just as I remembered it. It does make sense. It makes me stop to think. I'm not sure I understand it all, but I can ask Iglesiette about it later. "Yoda" is talking again. I guess I really should call him Pastor Bill. That's what the map calls him. *Pastor.* That must be some kind of title like *doctor* or *judge.* I wouldn't want him to take out my tonsils, but he does seem to know a lot about that book, the Bible.

He seems pretty upbeat. He smiles a lot. I think I like him. He's explaining what the words in the Bible mean. Like I couldn't figure it out by myself! Oh, well, I guess I never would have thought of it that way unless he mentioned it. He just told a joke. Is it okay to laugh here? I'm starting to feel at home.

Here it comes—the collection plate. Even I know what that is. What would happen if I didn't put anything in? Would they arrest me? Would I be kicked out of here? Would the lady behind me go "Tsk, tsk"? Great! Wouldn't you know it? I don't have anything smaller than a twenty. I think I can fake it. Iglesiette is whispering in my ear. She says no contribution is necessary. I should just consider myself a guest. Whew!

More music. Whoa! Now what? Everyone else seems to know the routine. They are walking up to the front and—is that food they're eating? There seem to be tiny glasses involved, too. No way do I want to make a fool of myself, but no one else is staying in their seats. I'm getting real nervous. Iglesiette is whispering again. She says she'll wait with me so I can watch. Thank goodness! I don't understand that whole bit at all. I do like watching, though. What do those Iglesiacs get out of it? It looks like bread; it smells like wine. What's so special about that? Yet they come back to their benches looking like they have seen the face of God Himself. I want to find out more about that.

The pastor is praying out loud. He's mentioning people I've heard of. I didn't know Iglesiette's mother was in the health-care unit. The pastor seems to care about her and her family. So do I. I've got to remember to send flowers, or whatever it is they send on this planet.

Amen. That means it's over. I'm a fast learner. I survived. Shake hands again, and ... Lunch? Iglesiette is asking me to join her and a few friends at the local buffet. Why not? Next week? Well, so many have invited me I guess it would be rude not to agree. Besides, I just promised that guy in the purple shirt that I'd sit with his kids and help keep them quiet during the service. I don't think they could do without me. I might ask my wife to come, too. I'd like to show her around.

You have cultivated a friendship. You have shared your story about your relationship with your Lord. You have introduced your friend to fellow Christians. You have invited your friend to join you in worship at your local church. Now what?

What kind of impression will your unchurched friend get the first time he or she joins you in your church? Will it seem like another planet, or will it feel comfortable and familiar? To a large extent, the answer to that question is out of your hands. Some churches are committed to making newcomers feel welcome; others feel it is important to do things according to well-established procedures and let visitors become educated to the ways of the church.

In this session we will identify strategies for assimilating the formerly unchurched or "dechurched" into the congregational family. First, you need to ascertain where the best placement will be for your friend. Although denominational loyalties are important, what is *most* important is that your friend become actively involved in a community of faith in which the Gospel is preached in its truth and purity and in which new Christians are nourished and loved. What is a church like that like?

Such a church, first of all, makes it a point to know what visitors need and want. Research indicates that unchurched people who attend a church for the first time are interested in discovering four basic things:

1. Doctrine and beliefs. They do not care about the finer points of confession, but they do want to know that they are not getting involved in a cult or non-Christian organization.

2. Denominational affiliation. It is in vogue today to downplay the fact that a congregation is affiliated with a mainstream denomination for fear of alienating those have had a negative experience with traditional church bodies. In fact, a church's denominational affiliation is no secret. Some dechurched people do have a bias against the denomination in which they were raised. Others feel at home with familiar settings from which they have drifted over the years.

3–4. Location and schedule. When the unchurched decide to attend, they do not want to stand out. They want to arrive on time without getting lost and blend in with the rest of the group. They do not particularly care how many members a church has; they care if a person they know is there. They typically feel most comfortable in a congregation of about 200 members—large enough to blend in without notice and small enough to care about individuals. Surprisingly, not many prospective attendees expressed any interest in a preview of the sermon topic, the qualifications of the pastor, or the availability of child care. It is assumed that all of these elements will be provided and will be of high quality.

When adults visit a church, they do not want to be treated differently than any other attendees. They do not like to wear name tags or be identified during the service. They merely want to blend in and observe. They do like to be greeted individually after the service by church members on an informal basis. They like information about the church to be readily available for them to research on their own terms. They enjoy participating in a voluntary church-sponsored reception after the service, and they appreciate receiving a thank-you note from the pastor during the week following their visit.

Visitors do not like being visited, unannounced, during the week, however. They do not appreciate being given a small gift brought to their home as a thank-you for attending, and they are not impressed by impersonal mass-marketing techniques.

Statistics show that during a given year about 7 percent of the nonchurched will sample a church. The single best way to reinforce a visitor's favorable impression and encourage their future attendance is for the one who invited that person to express gratitude that the person did, indeed, come. Interviews revealed only two items were found to have a positive effect on people's likelihood of attending a church—being invited by a trusted friend and attending interesting high-quality church sponsored events.

We are, of course, talking about general characteristics and likelihoods here. Your friend may be completely opposite of these descriptions. The key is to be ready to accept, know, and serve each friend individually.

Interested in Joining?

You have invited your friend, and your friend has expressed an interest in joining your church. How can you and your congregation now continue to support and nourish your friend's spiritual growth?

It is the Holy Spirit, of course, who is responsible for the preservation of faith in any Christian and for the growth and strength of any congregation. But the Holy Spirit has chosen to work through means in order to accomplish His purposes. He uses the people of God in every locale to nurture and support His family. He uses you.

Yet there are strong indicators that the extent to which new church members develop friendships in the congregation determines whether or not they will remain active or whether they will drop out of membership within the first few months. A study by Flavil Yeakley revealed the following information regarding 50 people who remained active in a church 6 months after joining and 50 people who dropped out within 6 months of joining.

No. of Friends	0	1	2	3	4	5	6	7	9	9+
Actives	0	0	0	1	2	2	8	13	12	12
Dropouts	8	13	14	8	4	2	1	0	0	0

From *The Master's Plan for Making Disciples* by Win and Charles Arn. Copyright © 1982 by Church Growth Press, Monrovia, CA. Used by permission.

Six seems to be the definitive number; 90 percent of the active members had six or more friends in the congregation; 98 percent of the dropouts had fewer than six friends.

People who have been members of a congregation for many years often do not realize the importance of such friendships. Because they are involved in a circle of long-time friends, they assume new members are also feeling accepted. They initially welcome new members, but they are reluctant to include them fully in their intimate fellowship.

There are two main avenues through which new members can become integrated into a congregation:

1. Joining a small group either before or immediately after becoming a member of the church
2. Accepting a formal role or office or being assigned an essential task in the congregation

These avenues bring the new member into interaction with church members and make them feel an important part of the church's ministry.

Tina started coming to church when her five-year old daughter, Marissa, a student in a public kindergarten, was asked to bring a picture to school of her best friend. Marissa brought a picture of Jesus. She had learned about Jesus in a church preschool, but when it was time to move to the elementary grades, her family saw no need to continue in a Lutheran school. Marissa's act of faith caused Tina to realize how important Jesus was to Marissa and how she had been neglecting the spiritual growth of her daughter. She brought Marissa to Sunday school and, while she was there, she began playing the piano for the Sunday school openings. Tina was a professional pianist—just the person the congregation had been looking for to accompany the singing at the contemporary service. Friends Tina had met in the congregation encouraged her to play. She enjoyed getting together to rehearse, and was soon playing every Sunday. When she became pregnant with her second child, she pointed to her unborn baby and remarked to her friend, "Look, another little Lutheran." At that time she had not officially joined the church, but she considered herself a member, and she soon formally became one.

Tina was loved into the fellowship of the church. She became a part of the group of parents and then musicians. She was given an important task, and her efforts were appreciated.

By the way, Tina had a friend who was also a musician, a singer. She invited him to join the group that sang at the contemporary service. He sang for several months and decided to bring his family. They are now members of the congregation, too. In fact, he has become a congregational leader. He loves to tell the story of his relationship with his Lord and is able to do so often. The cycle continues. A friend brings a friend, who brings a friend …

Joan had a similar experience, which ended differently. She first attended services out of curiosity—just shopping for a church. Although the congregation she visited is normally visitor-oriented and friendly, Joan seemed to slip through the cracks. For whatever reason, she did not feel welcome. When the pastor called on the phone during the week, Joan mentioned her impression. "Give us another chance," suggested the pastor. And she did. This time she was welcomed warmly. Greeters shook her hand. Members struck up conversations on the patio. She liked the service but had questions about doctrines and beliefs. The pastor invited her to attend the adult information class, and, as a result, Joan became a member.

Part of this congregation's assimilation plan is to get new members involved as soon as possible. A Sunday school teacher training class was beginning, and Joan decided she would give it a try. She was a little overwhelmed by the responsibility, but she was soon given a class to teach, which she enjoyed. There was not a lot of interaction among the teachers, however. She faithfully taught her class every week, but she missed the camaraderie of the teacher-training group. She was no longer the "newcomer," who received a lot of attention. People were still friendly, but there was no depth to the relationships. Joan decided this may not be the congregation for her after all.

She visited other churches for a while, then returned, then left again. What happened? She didn't dislike the church. She just never felt truly a part of it.

How would having a close friend in the church have helped? First, ideally, that friend would have accompanied her on her first visit. She would have introduced her personally to the pastor and other members. She would have shared the worship experience and told her she was glad she had come.

A friend might have gone with her to the information class and been able to continue the discussions in less formal settings, reinforcing and exploring the topics in more depth. The friend might have included Joan in a small group of which she was already a part. If Sunday school teaching was what Joan wanted to do, the friend might have been willing to assist. She would have been available to share frustrations and offer advice. She would have been there to hear about successes and the humorous incidents that occurred.

She would have been available during the week, also, to shop or carpool or talk on the phone. And she would have looked for

Joan each Sunday, eager to see her and worship with her.

If all those friendly involvements would have been happening, do you think Joan would still be a part of this congregation? Probably. If she still decided to move on, at least the friend would continue to keep in touch and, perhaps, provide the bridge back in the future. Or the friend could provide encouragement to Joan as she sought out a Christ-centered, Bible-based congregation.

Six friends might be better than one friend, but never underestimate the effectiveness of even one.

When you bring your friend to church, what will she find there? Rate the following suggestions with a 3 for absolutely essential, 2 for extremely helpful, 1 for nice but not necessary, or 0 for makes no difference.

____ Greeters shake hands at the door

____ Visitor parking area close to door

____ Clearly marked signs showing location of sanctuary, rest rooms, Bible classes

____ Short sermons

____ Traditional church hymns

____ Contemporary Christian songs

____ Liturgy printed out in service folder

____ Bible studies for newcomers

____ Coffee after the service

____ Visitor cards or sign-in book

____ Special service each week just for newcomers

____ Cards to indicate requests for prayer for this visitor

____ Clean, well-kept church and property

____ Reverent atmosphere

____ Informal atmosphere

____ Child care available

____ Service during the week instead of on Sunday

____ Chance to shake hands, pass peace, greet others during the service

____ Prayer groups that meet to pray for individuals they are befriending

____ other _____

____ other _____

____ other _____

Will everyone in your congregation give these suggestions the same ratings you did? Will the ratings be the same for congregations in different parts of the country or even different parts of the city? Will the ratings depend on the personality of the visitor you have in mind?

How can one church possibly be all thing to all people? Let's take a look at what was happening in some churches mentioned in the Bible.

Hebrews 9 presents an interesting comparison between worship in the Old and New Testament times. The Old Testament worship was intended to center around sacrifice and prayer. The tabernacle, later the magnificent temple, represented God's presence among His people. There was a clear delineation as to who could be included and where they were to be permitted as the entire worship experience symbolized the sacrifice of Jesus, who was to come. Gentiles and women could worship only in the outer courts. Converts and proselytes were accepted only if they followed the strict religious codes which designated who was a member of God's family and who was not. God planned the building, wrote the liturgy, and established practices and procedures. God used this model to picture the uniqueness of His kingdom and His relationship with His people. Social interaction between Jews and Gentiles was unlikely, but in the courtyard of the temple, all were equal in God's eyes—all were equally sinful; all needed a Savior; all needed a mediator in order to stand before the mighty God.

The word *church* first appears in the New Testament. No longer is worship confined to a particular building with particular rubrics. Christ has come! The shadow has become reality! God's people are free to *be* the royal priesthood formerly restricted to designated go-betweens. God's family has expanded. Membership is no longer a matter of genetics; it is a matter of faith.

Acts 2:42–47 describes what life was like in the early church:

> They devoted themselves to the apostles' teaching and to the fellowship, to the breaking of bread and to prayer. Everyone was filled with awe, and many wonders and miraculous signs were done by the apostles. All the believers were together and had everything in common. Selling their possessions and goods, they gave to anyone as he had need. Every day they continued to meet together in the temple courts. They broke bread in their homes and ate together with glad and sincere hearts, praising God and enjoying the favor of all the people. And the Lord

added to their number daily those who were being saved.

Would you join such a congregation? Would you bring a friend? You bet!

Why?

1. The Word of God was preached there—straight from the mouths of the apostles themselves, as they later wrote in the words of Scripture.

2. Friends were present—that special bond that we call "fellowship." This relationship was more than a "How are you? I'm fine" kind of contact. It was a heart to heart connection.

3. The Sacraments were being administered—the "breaking of bread." There is power in the Word and the Sacraments. These people were connected to their God in real and tangible ways. They were obedient to His directives and open to His blessings.

4. This was a place of prayer—for their own needs and the needs of others, regularly and openly, with thanksgiving.

5. God's presence was experienced with awe. There were no empty rituals or mindless repetitions. Along with the objective proclamation of the Gospel came the response of personal faith.

6. God's power was evident. Miracles happened. Sick people got well. Sad people experienced joy. Broken relationships were healed.

7. Love was expressed—unselfishly. People in need were being helped. This was a place where all were welcome—rich and poor—and where all had the opportunity to give. Offering plates would have been too small to contain the gifts so freely and lavishly donated. No fund-raising drives were needed.

8. They met regularly at the temple courts. They knew their roots. The temple where they had honored the coming Messiah now became the place to celebrate His presence. That was where their friends were who had not yet made the connection. They, too, could join in.

9. They got together socially—the first potlucks—good food, good talk, good times. They liked each other and thanked God for one another.

10. They accepted newcomers into their fellowship. It was God who had done the saving. They just opened their arms and homes and included them in the group.

If your church is like that, thank God. If you see areas that could be improved, thank God for that, too, and ask for His guidance in making things better. But don't give up.

When we invite friends to our homes we want everything to look its best. We dust and vacuum and clear the counters so everything looks perfect. We allow only family and close friends to see us as we really are. We don't live in model homes where there are no signs of real life. Real people leave their shoes in the middle of the floor and dirty cups next to the sink. Real people put fingerprints on the door sill and spill milk on the rug. Family members and close friends realize this. They like us just the way we are. They probably don't even see the evidences of real life we look at as flaws.

In the same way, we want our churches to look perfect to those we invite as guests. But churches are made up of real people. Real people sometimes hurt each others' feelings and are insensitive. Real people forget names and sing too loud. Real pastors preach boring sermons sometimes, and real church services sometimes last too long. Real church members live by the forgiveness of sins—their own and others.

Be sure your friend knows that you realize that the church of which you are a member is not perfect. Invite him or her to see you as a family member or close friend. If the basics are in place—the Word is taught in its truth and purity and the Gospel is proclaimed and lived—then smudges on the woodwork can be dealt with. Invite your friend to be part of the process.

If your church is not a comfortable one for your friend to associate with, help him or her find a Christian church that is.

What is important is that by the power of the Holy Spirit your friend has been led to recognize the power of sin, the need for a Savior, and the fact that Jesus is that Savior. When your friend has received Jesus personally and has joined into friendships with other Christians, affiliating with a Christian congregation will, along with your continued friendship and support, provide ongoing nurture, strength, and encouragement to live a lifestyle that glorifies God and helps other people.

WELCOME TO THE FAMILY

How Is It Going?

The focus of this book has been bringing your unchurched friends into fellowship with their Lord and His church. How is it going? Have you experienced the joy and excitement of seeing the results of your ministry? Or are you stuck at one of the early phases?

Don't give up. Your friendship with an unchurched friend is, in itself, a worthwhile commitment. Jesus did not reserve His care for only His followers. We see Him always busy healing, feeding, teaching everyone and anyone with whom He came in contact. He was known as the Friend of tax collectors and sinners. He, too, did not always see results. But His life showed the *process* of ministry.

You, too, are called upon to listen, teach, and care in Jesus' name—to extend His friendship through your words and actions.

Jesus explains it most clearly in John 15:12–17:

> My command is this: Love each other as I have loved you. Greater love has no one than this, that he lay down his life for his friends. You are My friends if you do what I command. I no longer call you servants, because a servant does not know his master's business. Instead, I have called you friends, for everything that I learned from My father I have made known to you. You did not choose Me, but I chose you and appointed you to go and bear fruit—fruit that will last. Then the Father will give you whatever you ask in My name. This is My command: Love each other.

Wow!

You have everything it takes to be a great friend; you have been befriended by the Master—God Himself. He asks no more of you than what He has already given to you—His unconditional love.

Seeking and nurturing a friendship is a time-consuming commitment. You already have a full schedule. You will have to give up a part of your life. That's probably the hardest part. Only a great lover would be willing to take on that kind of responsibility. God has made *you* a great lover.

Keep your eyes open. This is not a routine chore to be performed blindfolded. Not just anyone can do it. You are in on the task force, the planning commission. You see the big picture. You have the ultimate goal in mind. You have ownership in the process.

You did not pick up this book by accident. God chose *you* for this task. He will make you productive.

O my very dear friend,
How much I want to bear your burden,
   to share your trouble!
But I can only pray that God may be
   very close to you ...
   and keep you and protect you. ...
May He remember that you are His own,
   that you have dedicated your life to Him,
   that your heart's desire is to serve and please Him.
May He reach out to touch you ...
   may He fulfill your crying need in this hour.
And may we soon rejoice together over His deliverance
   and walk together in His service. (Psalm 20)

To Consider and Discuss

1. In what ways is worshiping in a church for the first time like visiting another planet? Which aspects are particularly stressful? How can you help newcomers feel welcome?

2. Do you agree that most active members of a church have at least six friends in the congregation? What is it about the number six that seems to make a difference?

3. Analyze Tina and Joan's experiences as described this session. What factors contributed to the final outcomes?

4. Discuss with someone in this class or with another member of your congregation the factors you rated as desirable when bringing your unchurched friend to visit. Do

you agree? Why or why not? Are these factors already in place? If not, what could you do to make them happen?

5. As the years have gone by, do you think churches today look more or less like the early model described in Acts 2? Why?

6. How is your church like the one mentioned in Acts? How is it different? What could you do to make it more like the early Christian church?

7. What has been the hardest part for you as you have worked at bringing a friend to Christ? What has been the easiest? Why?

8. Which specific words of encouragement in John 15 are particularly meaningful to you? Memorize them. Tell a friend about them.

9. Identify your next unchurched friend. Begin praying for that person and for opportunities to introduce that person to the Lord.

10. Make an appointment with your pastor (or invite your pastor to your class) to discuss your efforts at being a friend to an unchurched person. Tell him what you appreciate about your congregation and discuss areas that you feel should be evaluated. Thank him for faithfully proclaiming God's Word to you, and pray for him and his family.